Amazing grace

ELIZABETH VIERA TALBOT

Cover design by Gerald Lee Monks
Inside design by Kristin Hansen-Mellish
Cover resources from iStockphoto.com
Outside editor: Aivars Ozolins, PhD

Copyright © 2014 by Pacific Press® Publishing Association
Printed in the United States of America
All rights reserved

The author assumes full responsibility for the accuracy of all facts and quotations as cited in this book.

Unless otherwise indicated, Scripture quotations are taken from the *NEW AMERICAN STANDARD BIBLE*®, copyright © 1960, 1962, 1963, 1968, 1971, 1972, 1973, 1975, 1977, 1995 by The Lockman Foundation. Used by permission.

Scriptures quoted from NIV are from THE HOLY BIBLE, NEW INTERNATIONAL VERSION®, NIV®. Copyright © 1973, 1978, 1984, 2011 by Biblica, Inc.™ Used by permission. All rights reserved worldwide.

Portions of this material are taken from or based on previously published books by the author and are not otherwise cited. Those works include the following:

Surprised by Love, copyright © 2010 by Pacific Press® Publishing Association

Matthew: Prophecy Fulfilled, copyright © 2009 by Pacific Press® Publishing Association

Mark: Good News! copyright © 2012 by Pacific Press® Publishing Association

Luke: Salvation for All, copyright © 2012 by Pacific Press® Publishing Association

John: God Become Flesh, copyright © 2010 by Pacific Press® Publishing Association

Revelation: The Fifth Gospel, copyright © 2014 by Pacific Press® Publishing Association

Experiencing God's Love, chapter 6, "Love Never Ends," copyright © 2012 by Pacific Press® Publishing Association

Surprised by Love Women's Bible Study Guide, copyright © 2013 by Pacific Press® Publishing Association

You can obtain copies of these books by calling toll-free 1-800-765-6955 or by visiting www.adventistbookcenter.com. You can purchase them as eBooks by visiting www.adventist-ebooks.com.

Library of Congress Cataloging-in-Publication Data:
Talbot, Elizabeth Viera.
  Amazing grace / Elizabeth Viera Talbot.
    pages cm
  ISBN 13: 978-0-8163-5622-5 (pbk.)
  ISBN 10: 0-8163-5622-X (pbk.)
  1. Bible—Textbooks. 2. Grace (Theology)—Biblical teaching. 3. God (Christianity)—Love—Biblical teaching. I. Title.
  BS605.3.T35 2014
  234—dc23
                                    2014021344

October 2014

Contents

	Introduction	5
LESSON 1	Amazing *Plan*	7
LESSON 2	Amazing *Beauty*	13
LESSON 3	Amazing *Promise*	20
LESSON 4	Amazing *Kinship*	27
LESSON 5	Amazing *Faithfulness*	34
LESSON 6	Amazing *Rescue*	41
LESSON 7	Amazing *Love*	48
LESSON 8	Amazing *Assurance*	55
LESSON 9	Amazing *Reunion*	62
LESSON 10	Amazing *Restoration*	70
	An Invitation	78
	Bibliography	79

Amazing grace! How sweet the sound
That saved a wretch like me.
I once was lost, but now am found,
Was blind, but now I see.

—John Newton

Introduction

Dear Friend:

I am so excited to have you with me on this journey through the Bible. The *amazing grace* of God is absolutely outrageous, and we will study it all through eternity! Yet it is important to get started now in order to begin experiencing the peace and joy of salvation through Jesus Christ, our Lord!

Every time I try to describe the grace of God, I am reminded of how inadequate I am for that task, and how limited my words and thoughts are to explain the mystery of redemption! Nevertheless, we are embarking on a journey of utmost importance: seeking to get a better glimpse of God's love for us, trying to understand what would make Him give up heaven to save us, His beloved children. Why did He simply refuse to go through eternity without us?

Perhaps we can get a glimpse of God's *amazing grace* if we think of loving parents holding their baby for the very first time, right there making a silent covenant to protect and nurture this little one, created in their image, no matter what the cost might be. But what would the parents do if their beloved child were taken from them by a kidnapper, determined to destroy the baby eternally? Well . . . if you can imagine the answer to this question, then you can also begin to understand the desperation of God to get you back, the desperation that is narrated from Genesis to Revelation, His plan to successfully rescue you to be with Him forever.

A few years ago, the world experienced an unprecedented event that serves as a metaphor of God's salvation plan:

The flawless plan proceeded with incredible speed and remarkable efficiency. The rescue of all thirty-three miners trapped under seven hundred thousand tons of rock put an end to the longest underground entrapment in the history of the world. The saga, which started on August 5, 2010, when the mine collapsed, dragged on for sixty-nine days as the world watched spellbound in solidarity with the Chilean people and its government, while the rescuers continued their relentless efforts. Can you imagine being alive, nearly half a mile underground (2,041 feet), knowing that there is absolutely nothing you could do to get out? Help could only come from above, and it did. No cost was too great. It was after seventeen days with no contact with the miners that the word that they were still alive circled the globe. For fifty-two days after that the country placed all of its resources in bringing the trapped miners to the surface. Nothing like this had ever been successfully attempted before. Meanwhile, the men underground had only two choices: faith or fear. And they chose faith over fear.

On October 12, global audiences in the hundreds of millions—myself included—watched the live TV images showing the first rescuer arriving at the bottom, filmed by the miners. Just over twenty-four hours later, *all* thirty-three miners and all the rescuers were on the surface, celebrating in joy beyond words. "I can't describe the joy we are all feeling right now," said one of the miners. I can't even describe what I felt, and I was just watching it on TV! Two words kept coming up in the interviews that followed: *all* and *joy*. *All* had been rescued: the healthy and the sick, the strong and the weak. *All* had been saved through the plan designed from above. The resolution of the rescuers to reach the trapped miners overcame all the obstacles they found. And at the end, only pure *joy* remained. *All* had been saved from sure death.

The Bible was written to announce a rescue of even greater magnitude! The human race was buried under sin, with no possibility of eternal survival. Help could only come from above. "And it did!" announce the biblical writers in the most excited tones. The Savior of the world came down to fulfill Heaven's plan to rescue the world! As you can imagine, the Scriptures are filled with joy and excitement, because no cost was too great for Heaven, and salvation has been achieved *for all who accept His plan, believing in the Master Rescuer and His amazing grace!*

If you would like to have a couple of books to guide you as we go through these studies together, let me suggest the *Jesus 101* devotional book series I wrote based on the witness to Jesus' life, death, and resurrection found in the four Gospels. And as we get to the last three lessons in this course, I think you would really enjoy another one of my booklets, *Revelation: The Fifth Gospel,* which offers the final victorious view of Jesus as the King of Kings, as He achieves the ultimate restoration. The whole Bible may truly be summarized in just two words: JESUS WINS!

So, are you getting excited? Are you ready? Well . . . I can't wait to get started because I know that very soon our souls will be on fire and will be singing a new song! A new song prompted by the MEGA JOY of a redeemed heart! Let's get started and bask in His *amazing grace*! Woo-Hoo!

Pastor Elizabeth Talbot, PhD
Speaker/Director
www.Jesus101institute.com

Amazing Plan

Lesson 1

Read Genesis 1:1–19, 26–31, and as you read the biblical narrative, highlight words or phrases that catch your attention.

Let's study

"In the beginning God created the heavens and the earth" (Genesis 1:1). The seven Hebrew words that make up the first sentence in the Scriptures foreshadow the seven days of the creation process. God was preparing a *perfect* place for His children; they were the crown of His creation. As God was speaking their home into existence, He was also making qualitative statements about how well things were going. After the second day, "It was good" is found at the completion of every day, signifying that God was pleased with how earth was becoming the ideal home for *His babies*. Each day starts with "then God said," and it ends with "there was evening and there was morning." Every day God gave a command, and the narrative highlights the accomplishment of each command as we get closer and closer to *the day* when His children would arrive.

And then . . .

It was time! God was about to create His children—His babies. From this moment on, everything would be different. His universe would change forever. Their home was ready, the day had arrived. And God paused.

A divine council took place *exclusively* before creating humankind in the Creation narrative. As God is dialoguing in community, we get a glimpse of the uniqueness and climactic significance of this moment: "Then God said, 'Let Us make man' " (Genesis 1:26). "Man" (*'adam*) is a collective name for humankind, as will be further explained in Genesis 1:27. God has reflected and decided to have children. You can almost picture in your mind a husband and wife in intimate conversation at the kitchen table, planning the most important decision of their lives: "Let's have children."

God's children would be in His image: "Let Us make man in Our image, according to Our likeness" (verse 26). Humankind would bear God's image and likeness; humans would be like God but not identical to God; in His image and likeness, but not gods. God had made the decision. In Genesis 1:26, we hear the voice of God in the first person. Then the narrator poetically reports the creation of God's children in the third person, emphasizing that we were created in His image: "God created man in His own image, in the image of God He created him; male and female He created them" (verse 27).

Humankind is created in the image of the Sovereign Creator, and as such, God delegates His sovereignty and now His children are to rule the earth. They hold the highest place in the created order. Are you feeling pretty special by now?

Well, God thinks that His children are more than special. When He evaluates His creative work of the sixth day, He can't just call it "good" as in all the other days. No! The plants and the animals are good, the children are VERY GOOD! "God saw all that He had made, and behold, it was *very good*. And there was evening and there was morning, the sixth day" (verse 31; emphasis added). Yes, having a garden is *good,* having a pet is *good*. But having children is *very good*! This was *the* day they came to life, and God would always remember it, the way you remember the day your child was born. That was the most important day in your life! And it was *very good*!

> Fill in the blanks with your own name:
> "Then God said, 'Let Us make _____ in Our image, according to Our likeness; and let _____ rule over the fish of the sea and over the birds of the sky and over the cattle and over all the earth, and over every creeping thing that creeps on the earth.' God created _____ in His own image, in the image of God He created _____" (Genesis 1:26, 27).

Let's understand

Image of God: In the ancient cultures of Egypt and Mesopotamia, the designation of being "in the image of God" was reserved exclusively for prominent people: kings, important officers, and royal rulers. The Genesis narrative emphasizes that God did not make such distinctions. When God decided to create mankind in His own image, He did not make some people more special than the others—He did not separate them by hierarchy and power. *Every human being* bears the image of God. The royal language is used for every child of God, regardless of status, caste, gender, or position in society. YOU are a child of God! We are His royal children!

The concept of the *image of God* is so special that it appears only four times in Jewish Scripture and always in relation to the creation of humankind (see Genesis 1:26, 27 [twice]; 9:6). The Hebrew verb *'bara* ("create") is used only with God as the subject. He creates children, male and female (*'adam*), in His image, according to His likeness. Each gender is given unique characteristics that together make a complete, comprehensive, and complementary view of God. We are all created in the image of God!

Only the biblical Creation speaks of a God who serenely makes man in His own image to be part of His divine family. Only the biblical Creation rehearses the story of a supreme Godhead who deliberately creates humans for the purpose of fellowship. Only the biblical Creation recalls that humans are given rulership of the earth as God's representatives.

Later Seth is described as being "in his [Adam's] own likeness, according to his image" (Genesis 5:3). God had children in His image; Adam had children in his image; and you have children in YOUR image! Perhaps you are already beginning to understand the plan of redemption . . . and we haven't even started yet.

Divine Dialogue: "Then God said, 'Let Us make . . .' " (Genesis 1:26). This is the only "divine dialogue" in the Creation account. The Godhead planning to create the human race: "Before undertaking the next act of creation God took counsel. This unique reference to God's reflecting in community before making something underscores both the importance and the uniqueness of what God was about to create" (Hartley, *Genesis,* p. 47).

Selfless Community: God, who is love and exists in the selfless, intimate community of Three Persons in One, was about to create a race to love and cherish: humankind. God wanted to give humans the capacity to love selflessly too, so that they might understand His love better. And because God exists in the intimate community that we call Trinity, He intended that a woman and a man also would exist in an intimate community that we call marriage: "For this reason a man shall leave his father and his mother, and be joined to his wife; and they shall become *one* flesh" (Genesis 2:24; emphasis added). I think it is extremely important and revealing that the Hebrew word used for "one" in this verse is the same word used in the Shema when describing the "oneness" of God: "Hear, O Israel! The Lord is our God, the Lord is *one*!" (Deuteronomy 6:4; emphasis added). The *Shema* (Hebrew for "hear"), found in Deuteronomy 6:4–9, is the Jewish confession of faith, and is recited daily. God is one God, existing in community, as a man and a woman are one flesh. Perhaps now humankind would understand God's selfless love for them a little bit better.

Let's reflect

What would you do for your child? Let me tell you what my parents did for me.

Suffering is hard enough. But when in addition to suffering you also feel alone, it is easy to fall into hopelessness. I remember a particular Christmas, many, many years ago. It was a difficult and lonely season in my life. This was a dark, cold loneliness, a time of helplessness and of unspeakable pain. It was a time of mourning, the type that takes a long time to process, because dreams die slowly and painfully. It wasn't helping that this was the holiday season, a time of family togetherness and celebration. Deep inside, in my soul, in that sacred place where no one else is allowed to enter, I was feeling ALONE, terribly ALONE! My parents, who had always been very supporting and loving, lived on the East Coast of the United States, while I lived on the other coast, in California. Neither my parents nor I had enough money to visit the other for Christmas that year. So they had planned to spend it in Maryland, and I would be alone, with only my thoughts and questions for company.

But then something incredible happened! I received good news, something that I couldn't have possibly imagined! An airline decided to advertise a very inexpensive special fare just for Christmas. However, the promotion came with a very specific restriction: The trip both ways had to be completed within a window of forty-eight hours, on December 24 and 25. I understand that a one-day visit like this would make sense for anyone who lived within an hour or two of their loved ones. But who would cross the whole country, flying six hours each way in less than forty-eight hours? Well . . . MY PARENTS did! They called me to announce excitedly that both of them were coming to spend Christmas together with me! They would arrive on December 24 and leave the following evening. WOW! I can't even describe what I felt! How could anyone love me that much and come all this distance just to let me know that I was NOT alone? I will never forget that Christmas. I remember every detail about it. I was not alone after all . . . someone loved me and cared for me deeply. Sometimes love and suffering require extraordinary and unexpected measures. God would demonstrate His love for us in a most surprising manner . . .

Write a story from your own daily life that comes to your mind in this session:

How does it make you feel that the whole earth was created for you?
_____

How do the gifts of beauty and love from the Master Designer affect you?
_____

What does it mean to you when Jesus calls you "My child"?

Repeat these words of Scripture together:

> *"See how great a love the Father has bestowed on us,*
> *That we would be called children of God;*
> *And such we are"* (1 John 3:1).

Let's comprehend Jesus in Scripture

GENESIS 1:1-5	JOHN 1:1-5
1 In the beginning God created the heavens and the earth.	1 In the beginning was the Word, and the Word was with God. . . .
2 The earth was formless and void, and darkness was over the surface of the deep, and the Spirit of God was moving over the surface of the waters.	2 He was in the beginning with God.
3 Then God said, "Let there be light"; and there was light.	3 All things came into being through Him and apart from Him nothing came into being that has come into being.
4 God saw that the light was good, and God separated the light from the darkness.	4 In Him was life, and the life was the Light of men.
5 God called the light day, and the darkness He called night. And there was evening and there was morning, one day.	5 The Light shines in the darkness, and the darkness did not comprehend it.

How many things do you find in common between the two texts?

Why do you think that John wanted us to have Genesis 1 in mind when he introduces us to Jesus in the first chaper of his Gospel?

Let's respond to God's amazing plan

Write a thanksgiving psalm or a prayer of gratitude to God for creating you in His image, for lovingly forming a beautiful world for your home. Thank Him for loving you with an everlasting love and promising that He will NEVER FORGET YOU!

*"Can a woman forget her nursing child
And have no compassion on the son of her womb?
Even these may forget, but I will not forget you.
Behold, I have inscribed you on the palms of My hands"*
(Isaiah 49:15, 16).

God's amazing plan was to create children in HIS IMAGE, to share the dominion of this world with them, to give them the ability to multiply and fill the earth, and to fellowship with them throughout eternity. That the Sovereign God of the universe would deliberately design us in His image is more than our minds can comprehend. He created us to be with Him forever! Yes, the Master planned you and me. We will live in awe of His *amazing* plan throughout eternity. And wait until you see what He went through to make His plan successful!

Do you believe and accept God's amazing plan for you? Take a moment to write a prayer of thanksgiving and acceptance to Him who loved you SO MUCH!

Amazing Beauty

Lesson 2

Read Genesis 2:1–25, and as you read the biblical narrative, highlight words or phrases that catch your attention.

Let's study

"The LORD God planted a garden toward the east, in Eden; and there He placed the man whom He had formed. Out of the ground the LORD God caused to grow every tree that is pleasing to the sight and good for food" (Genesis 2:8, 9). Oh, this was such a special nursery! God planted the beautiful Garden just for His babies' delight. He placed humans in this unique place that He had designed for them. Can you imagine God planting trees that were not just good for food, but pleasing to the sight so that His children would delight in the beauty that surrounded them? Just like you did for your children, who are in your image.

This nursery garden was the place of ultimate beauty. In the ancient Semitic language of the Mediterranean area, the root word for *Eden* means "delight." Furthermore, when the Jewish Scriptures (Old Testament) were translated into Greek, many years before Jesus Christ was born, the Greek word for "garden" utilized in Genesis 2:8, 9 was *paradeisos*. The Garden of Eden was, in the fullest sense of the expression, the "Paradise of delight." Of course! What else would God give His children?

In the midst of the *paradeisos,* God placed the "tree of life" (verse 9). The fruit of the tree of life was a visual and tactile reminder of the children's connection with the Life-Giver. They were created to be eternal, just as God is eternal. They would eat and live forever. That's who they were and that was the plan! We have eternity placed deep in the core of our souls, because we were made in the image of the Everlasting God.

Now that His children had come to life, the creation process was complete; it was done, finished, and perfect. It was time to celebrate! God ceased His work and blessed and sanctified the seventh day, the day that forever would point to the completeness and wholeness of God's creation. The seventh day would be perpetually linked with Creation and redemption. But wait! We haven't discussed redemption yet. It's coming up in the next few chapters—and I can't wait to tell you about it!

Humans were the children of God. And as such, they spent the very first day of their lives together with the Creator in the special Garden made for them, celebrating the completeness of God's creation, of which they were the crowning masterpiece. The seventh day was *the* first day the Creator and His children spent together in intimate communion. "By the seventh day God completed His work which He had done, and He rested on the seventh day from all His work which He had done. Then God blessed the seventh day and sanctified it, because in it He rested from all His work which God had created and made" (verses 2, 3). The Creator and His creatures rested together. Wouldn't you have done the same? Don't you love to take time to celebrate together with your children? Well, God did not just want a birthday celebration once a year—He wanted us to remember every week, on the seventh day. So He set it apart and made it holy. His children would have a constant reminder that He was their Creator.

Fill in the blank with your own name:
"The Lord God planted a garden toward the east, in Eden; and there He placed _____ whom He had formed. Out of the ground the Lord God caused to grow every tree that is pleasing to the sight and good for food; the tree of life also in the midst of the garden, and the tree of the knowledge of good and evil" (Genesis 2:8, 9).

Let's understand

The Beauty of Paradise: "**God . . . planted a garden in the east, in Eden: and there he put the man.** The garden was located at the center of the earth, somewhere to the east of the narrator. In the garden God planted **all kinds of trees.** Trees represent the majestic beauty of the garden as well as providing **food,** shade and shelter for the animals. **In the middle of the garden** God planted **the tree of life** (2:15–17).

"A parenthetical paragraph [2:10–14] gives information either to anchor the garden of Eden to a definite geography, to place the origin of four great rivers in primeval time, or both. Rising from a huge spring fed by the great deep, the river flowed through Eden and then divided into **four** branches that brought water to the various quarters of the earth.

"Two of the rivers are **the Tigris** and **the Euphrates.** The identities of **the Pishon** and **the Gihon** are uncertain, but the Pishon carried water to **Havilah,** a part of southeastern Arabia, rich in **gold** (10:7, 29; 25:18; 1 Sam. 15:7; 1 Chron. 1:9, 23). Other valuable items, possible **aromatic resin and onyx** (the meaning of the Hebrew terms is unknown), were found there. This fact informs us that God provided an abundance of wealth on the earth" (Hartley, *Genesis,* p. 60).

"God provided an abundance of wealth on the earth." Compare this statement with Jesus' saying in John 10:10.

The Beauty of Freedom: Just as my parents lovingly protected me by instructing me not to engage in conversations with strangers or get into unknown cars, God gave His beloved children directions on how to stay away from harm. Because humans were created as moral beings, God would protect their freedom with a boundary, a very clear boundary. They would know exactly when they were crossing the line to moral independence. God gave them an umbrella permission with a prohibition that was the exception: "The LORD God commanded the man, saying, 'From any tree of the garden you may eat freely; but from the tree of the knowledge of good and evil you shall not eat, for in the day that you eat from it you will surely die' " (Genesis 2:16, 17). "Any tree" included the tree of life. Their default would be endless life, eating from all the other trees and the tree of life. But, if they chose to be like gods, thinking that they could discern what was good and what was evil, they would separate themselves from the Life-Giver's care and would be under the sentence of death. They were perfect moral beings who knew only good, but they could choose to leave God's umbrella of ethical discernment. To live or to die—that was their choice.

As any person who is in love would tell you, you can't hold your beloved hostage. Love simply can't exist without freedom; therefore, freedom to choose is a basic prerequisite for love to exist. If freedom is not in the equation, then love is turned into fear. That's why, aside from the tree that reminded them of God's eternal plan (the tree of life), there was another tree; it was called the tree of the knowledge of good and evil (verse 9). If they ever wanted to leave God and His moral umbrella, this was their way out.

The Beauty of Wholeness: "The declaration **they will become one flesh** describes further the unity of a man and a woman. The focus is not on the resulting sexual relationship or the children to be born, though it does not exclude these expressions of their union. Rather, the emphasis is on the spiritual and social unity of the new couple. In becoming one flesh a man and a woman become more closely bonded than their blood kinship. Because the deepest human relationship is found in marriage, any spouse's abuse or domination of the other denies their mutuality and disrupts the harmony God intended" (Hartley, *Genesis,* p. 64).

"The climax of the creation is, interestingly, the notation that the couple *were naked* and felt no shame before each other [Genesis 2:25]. Of course, *naked* refers primarily to physical nudity, but one may also think that no barrier of any kind drove a wedge between Adam and Eve" (Hamilton, *The Book of Genesis: Chapters 1–17,* p. 181).

Let's reflect

I know that many times during my youthful years I was undeserving of my parents' kindness, and yet they were compassionate and loving toward me. Many times I thought I knew better than they did. One day, in my early teens, instead of accepting my mother's help, I decided I would cut my own hair. So I locked myself in the bathroom and got busy. And then I experienced what is known in psychology as "escalation of commitment." I realized that something was wrong, but since I had already invested some energy and pride into the project, I kept going, trying to fix the problem. However, it went from bad to worse. Has that ever happened to you? You realize that you are going the wrong way, but by then you have invested money, time, honor, and skills so you stay the course, investing even more regardless of the obvious fact that it is getting you nowhere.

Very soon I realized that I was in deep trouble. I was trying to clean up the mess that I had created on my head, but my problem was that I was running out of hair to fix, and fast. I had only a few inches of hair left, much less than I had imagined at the beginning of my venture. And it was all uneven! Then it finally dawned on me that this would probably be a good time to go back to my mother's room, ask her for forgiveness (for rejecting her help), and become her slave for life (just kidding) if she could just make me look like a normal person again. Even though I thought I was beyond repair! I came out of the bathroom with a pair of scissors and a desperate look on my face. My mother had every right to reject me and to make me live with the consequences of my actions! But she asked me to sit on the kitchen chair, and with love and much skill, she spent a long, long time trying to make some semblance of respectability out of the little hair I had left. I ended up with a cute, *very* short haircut and a grateful soul.

So many times in my life I acted as though I knew better than God . . . I am stubborn, and yet He is patient, compassionate, and loving with me.

Write a story from daily life that comes to your mind in this session:

"Adam and Eve had no need of material clothing, for about them the Creator had placed a robe of light, a robe symbolic of His own righteous character, which was reflected perfectly in them" (*The Seventh-day Adventist Bible Commentary*, vol. 1, p. 227). In the history of redemption, what brought about the "clothing crisis"?

In the BEAUTY of God's moral umbrella, there was no shame. Why is there shame now?

Read Genesis 3:7. We will be dealing with the fall of humanity in our next lesson, but why do you think that the first thing Adam and Eve did when they sinned, and found themselves naked, was to sew fig leaves together to make coverings for themselves?

Why does the "clothing crisis" continue until the end of time? (See Revelation 3:17, 18.)

Repeat these words of Scripture together:

> *"I will rejoice greatly in the* LORD,
> *My soul will exult in my God;*
> *For He has clothed me with garments of salvation,*
> *He has wrapped me with a robe of righteousness"* (Isaiah 61:10).

Let's comprehend Jesus in Scripture

We will be addressing the theme of redemption in the following lessons. But it is very important for us to understand, at this point in the biblical narrative, that the *amazing beauty* of the completion of God's work applies not only to creation but to redemption as well, because He vowed to re-create the beauty that He originally designed for humanity. That is why many of the words and concepts we have studied in the first three chapters of Genesis regarding creation will be repeated in the New Testament in regard to the redemption brought about by Jesus. Consider the following insights from Genesis and the New Testament:

GENESIS	NEW TESTAMENT

Completion (Genesis 2:1, 2)

In these verses we are told that God "completed" creation. In the Greek version of the Old Testament (Septuagint, LXX), this word contains the verb *teleō*, which means to finish, complete, accomplish.

Completion (John 19:30)

The final cry of Jesus on the cross, dying to redeem the world, was, "It is finished!" This last statement of Jesus also contains the verb *teleō* ("to complete, finish, accomplish").

Rest and Sabbath (Genesis 2:2, 3)

The seventh day was set apart by God to become a memorial of Creation (see Exodus 20:8–11). God rested on this day, celebrating the completion of Creation. He blessed this day and sanctified it.

Rest and Sabbath (Hebrews 4:9, 10)

In Jesus, the seventh-day Sabbath becomes a celebration of our redemption as well. When the believer enters full rest by trusting Christ's redemptive work, that person rests from his own works, as God did from His in Creation.

Covering nakedness (Genesis 3:7, 21)

When Adam and Eve sinned, they found themselves naked and tried to hide their shame with coverings made from fig leaves. But God made garments of skin for them, and clothed them.

Covering nakedness (Revelation 3:17, 18)

Throughout the Bible, this "clothing crisis" is the choice between self-sufficiency and God's provision. Jesus Himself exhorts us to get our white garments from Him so that we may be clothed and the shame of our nakedness may not be revealed.

Paradise and Tree of Life (Genesis 2:8, 9; 3:24)

The beautiful place God prepared for His children was the paradise of delight. In the middle of this Garden was the ever-present reminder of their connection with the Life-Giver: the tree of life. Unfortunately, humans lost paradise and access to the tree of life, and became "mortals."

Paradise and Tree of Life (Revelation 2:7; 22:14)

Because Jesus would take humanity's death upon Himself, He re-opened the way to paradise (see Luke 23:43). Those who would believe in Jesus' death in their place would once again have access to the tree of life (Revelation 22:14) and eternity. The Bible starts and ends with the same theme. It is a full circle!

Let's respond to God's amazing beauty

Write a covenant between you and God to trade your shame for HIS wholeness. On the left side, make a list of all the things in your life that you want to trade. Then, on the right side, write what God will replace those things with. Follow the example on the first line.

"The Spirit of the Lord God is upon me, because the Lord has anointed me to bring good news to the afflicted; He has sent me to bind up the brokenhearted, to proclaim liberty to captives and freedom to prisoners. . . . Giving them a garland **instead** of ashes, the oil of gladness **instead** of mourning, the mantle of praise **instead** of a spirit of fainting. . . . **Instead** of your shame *you will have a* double *portion,* and instead *of* humiliation they will shout for joy" (Isaiah 61:1, 3, 7; emphasis added).

Instead of my:	God will give me His:
SHAME	**WHOLENESS**

God wanted His children to live surrounded with beauty and abundance. He even clothed them with His robe of righteousness and blessed them with a paradise of delight. Glimpses of the *amazing beauty* of His design may still be observed in the magnificence of nature all around us. And still, we can't imagine what it was at the beginning, before sin entered this world. Nevertheless, God did not give up when His children became trapped in a shameful "clothing crisis." He promised to rescue us and to bring us back to the paradise of delight. But the price would be very high, because our robes would be made white only in the blood of the Lamb (see Revelation 7:14)!

Do you believe and accept God's amazing beauty planned for you? Do you believe that you were created to be with God eternally? Take a moment to write a prayer of thanksgiving and acceptance to Him who created everything perfect just for you and now promises that you will be back in PARADISE because He gave His life as a ransom for you!

Amazing Promise

Lesson 3

Read Genesis 3:1–15, 21–24, and highlight words or phrases that catch your attention.

Let's study

The kidnapper and deceiver took upon himself the form of a serpent (see Genesis 3:1). This was an attractive sight because this animal was beautiful, and the first woman was mesmerized by it. She established a conversation with this beautiful animal without realizing that she was getting too close to trespassing over the protective boundary. Aside from the attractive beauty used by the deceiver, the kidnapper's tactics reflect well thought-out, crafty methods. The first sentence spoken by the serpent is an expression of shock! And it comes with an exaggeration of God's words: "Indeed, has God said, 'You [all of you, second person plural] shall not eat from any tree of the garden'?" (Genesis 3:1). Of course God had said exactly the opposite: they could eat of any tree in the Garden except for one (see Genesis 2:16, 17). Kidnappers have always been, and always will be, crafty deceivers.

Even though the kidnapper is having this conversation with Eve, the first woman (see Genesis 3:20), all the pronouns—*you* and *we*—are plural because she is being addressed as the representative of the first couple, and she is answering for herself, for her husband, and, ultimately, for humankind. She decides that she needs to "correct" the kidnapper, because his statement is not true (which should have been a hint of what was coming). The correction states, "From the fruit of the trees of the garden we may eat; but from the fruit of the tree which is in the middle of the garden, God has said, 'You shall not eat from it or touch it, or you will die' " (Genesis 3:2, 3). The kidnapper then makes a false assertion, just the opposite of what God had said. "The serpent said to the woman, 'You surely will not die!' " (verse 4). This is the greatest lie! God had said, "You will surely die" (Genesis 2:17). The deceiver then continues by explaining God's own thoughts, as if he were "unmasking" God's real motives: "For God knows that in the day you eat from it your eyes will be opened, and you will be like God, knowing good and evil" (Genesis 3:5). That was it! YOU can be gods, deciding for yourselves what is good and what is evil. You don't need the Creator anymore! You can have moral independence; you have discernment. Why are you putting up with all this mistreatment that is keeping you from your potential? You can do better than this!

Sound familiar?

The woman took another look at the tree: "When the woman saw that the tree was good for food, and that it was a delight to the eyes, and that the tree was desirable to make one wise . . ." (verse 6). Make one wise? Where did she get THAT from? Well, from the kidnapper, of course. Now God's little girl was thinking like the deceiver. And she reached out and . . . "took from its fruit and ate; and she gave also to her husband with her, and he ate" (verse 6). NO! Why did they think that was wisdom? Why didn't they stay with the Source of wisdom and life? The description of Eve's and Adam's sin is narrated in eight words in the Hebrew language. Just eight words that would change the history of the universe. Having talked to the kidnapper, Eve was tricked into believing that she could have moral discernment without God and would become "wiser."

So she ate the forbidden fruit, breaching the boundary of God's protection, and she went to her husband and he also ate. Hers was the sin of initiative; his was the sin of compliance, a tacit consent. God's children had been KIDNAPPED!

> Fill in the blanks with your own name:
> "_____ heard the sound of the LORD God walking in the garden in the cool of the day and hid from the presence of the LORD God among the trees of the garden. Then the LORD God called _____ and said, 'Where are you?' _____ said, 'I heard the sound of You in the garden, and I was afraid' " (Genesis 3:8–10, paraphrase).

One of the immediate consequences of sin was that human beings started to feel afraid of their Creator. Why do you think FEAR took over the children of God?

The Fall to Self-Sufficiency: The children of God chose to leave the moral umbrella of their Creator. They began believing in a lie, and sin entered our world. But the outcome was not what they were expecting; the grass looks greener on the other side, until you get there . . .

"Instead of knowing good and evil, the couple now know that they are naked. This is hardly the knowledge for which they bargained. What was formerly understood to be a sign of a healthy relationship between the man and the woman (2:25) has now become something unpleasant and filled with shame. Even the word for 'naked' in 2:25 is written a bit differently from the one that is used here [3:7].

"The couple's solution to this new enigma is freighted with folly. Having committed the sin themselves, and now living with its immediate consequences, i.e., the experience of shame, the loss of innocence (*they were aware that they were naked*), they attempt to alleviate the problem themselves. Rather than driving them back to God, their guilt leads them into a self-atoning, self-protecting procedure: they must cover themselves" (Hamilton, *The Book of Genesis,* p. 191).

Why do you think the couple's solution was to try to fix it themselves instead of going back to God? Do you think we still do that today?

The Pain: Aside from the fear, shame, and blame that resulted from the Fall, from now on men and women would experience pain. But the curse was on the serpent:

"God cursed the serpent and the ground. He did not curse the humans but inflicted pain in their efforts to sustain life, bearing children and producing food.... God therefore addressed **the serpent,** telling it that it was **cursed** and would **crawl on** its **belly** ... **and eat dust.** 'Eat dust' is a metaphor for the humiliation of the most exalted animal. From then on there would be **enmity between** the serpent and **the woman, between** the **offspring** of both....

"**To the woman** God **said** that he would **greatly increase** her **pains** (*'itsabon*) **in childbearing** [3:16]....

"Consequently, in working the ground to produce food for life, the man would experience pain (*'itsabon*) from his labor. This term for pain is the same as that for bearing children....

"Thus God did not hold one more blameworthy than the other" (Hartley, *Genesis,* pp. 69, 70).

Aside from pain, now humanity had become mortal: "For you are dust, and to dust you shall return" (Genesis 3:19).

We are told that all the consequences of the Fall will no longer be present in the new earth: "He will wipe away every tear from their eyes; and there will no longer be any death; there will no longer be any mourning, or crying, or pain; the first things have passed away" (Revelation 21:4).

What comes to your mind when you read Revelation 21:4?

The Promise: *Our story* would be the saddest and most hopeless story in the universe if the Bible had ended in Genesis 3:7. But that is not where the Bible ends! It's where it begins. Because in Genesis 3:15 we receive the first covenant that brings hope; the announcement that this was not the end:

"A few late Jewish writers and the church fathers found in this verse a fuller meaning that would one day be realized in the Messiah, when a representative of all humans would strike the serpent, the representative of the forces that oppose God, with a fatal blow. That victory would put an end to the enmity between the serpent and humankind. As Scripture unfolds God's design, it becomes clear that the one to achieve such a major victory is the Messiah" (Hartley, *Genesis,* p. 69).

This promise is the beginning of what is called "the covenant," the promise that God made to redeem His children from their mortal fall. The rest of the Bible will tell the story of redemption, and I can't wait to tell you about it! I am so excited! God loved His children SO MUCH that He surprised us all . . . we were kidnapped, but He surprised us with His indescribable love. He Himself would give up heaven in order to rescue us!

"God was in Christ reconciling the world to Himself, not counting their trespasses against them. . . . He made Him who knew no sin to be sin on our behalf, so that we might become the righteousness of God in Him" (2 Corinthians 5:19–21).

What is the most surprising part of His promise?

Let's reflect

When I was a little girl, my parents took me to a city in Argentina named Córdoba. My father, then a pastor, was attending workers' meetings in a hotel for a few days. My mother anticipated having a good time in the company of other pastors' wives, and we, the children, excitedly looked forward to spending every minute of the day playing in the hotel's swimming pool. I was three and was told in no uncertain terms that I was to stay in the shallow part of the pool at all times—NO EXCEPTIONS! The happy day finally arrived, and I found myself in water bliss. All of a sudden something unexpected happened to me. I found myself in water at the edge of the forbidden zone, and the bottom of the pool was very slippery. VERY SLIPPERY! Green and slimy. I started sliding toward the deep end of the pool as if I were in an underwater playground, except that this was no fun. I found myself exactly in the very place where my mother told me not to go; and now I knew, in my young three-year-old heart, that I would die because I had no way out. But there was something else that my heart knew—if my mother saw me, she would rescue me. Somehow, in my young brain, I understood that my mother's love for me would oblige her to jump in and save me. But the problem was that she couldn't see me! I gathered all my strength and tried to jump up, pushing my feet against the bottom of the pool, but I was already under the water and only my hand briefly appeared above the surface and then disappeared again. I tried it again and again. AND MY MOTHER SAW ME! Yes, she noticed my little fingers above the water—and that was all she needed!

SHE DIVED INTO THE POOL! It didn't matter what she was wearing or who was watching. All that mattered to her was that her little girl was drowning and she had to save her. And she did save me!

Write a story from daily life that comes to mind in this session:

Write down expressions of FEAR, SHAME, and BLAME found in Genesis 3:8–13.

Why do you think God did not abandon the human race when it rejected His moral umbrella?

Imagine and describe your first reunion with your Creator.

Repeat these words of Scripture together:

> *"Blessed are those who wash their robes, so that they may have the right to* the tree of life, *and may enter by the gates into the city. . . .*
> *The Spirit and the bride say, 'Come.' And let the one who hears say, 'Come.' And let the one who is thirsty come; let the one who wishes take the water of life without cost. . . .*
> *He who testifies to these things says, 'Yes, I am coming quickly.' Amen. Come, Lord Jesus"* (Revelation 22:14, 17, 20; emphasis added).

Let's comprehend Jesus in Scripture

Read Luke 24:25–49. In this story, Jesus explains how to interpret Scripture as a whole: "And He said to them, 'O foolish men and slow of heart to believe in all that the prophets have spoken! Was it not necessary for the Christ to suffer these things and to enter into His glory?' Then beginning with Moses and with all the prophets, He explained to them the things concerning Himself in all the Scriptures" (Luke 24:25–27). Somehow their unbelief had not allowed them to interpret the Scripture accurately! There was a plan! Christ HAD to go through this! And the plan was explained from the beginning of the Bible (Moses and all the Prophets).

The verb *to explain* (from the Greek *diermēneuō*) contains the root word for *hermeneutics,* which in English identifies the methodology of interpreting a biblical text. Here, Jesus provides the best biblical interpretive rule ever! All the Law of Moses and the Prophets are about Him! The two disciples got so excited that in "that very hour" (verse 33) they decided to go back to Jerusalem to tell everyone! They didn't feel their tired legs or the seven miles back. They just *had* to go back. When they got there, Jesus Himself shows up in the room! "Peace be to you" (verse 36). After spending a few moments with them and eating a broiled fish in front of them (verses 42, 43), Jesus starts the same explanation that He had given the two travelers, this time in more detail, repeating the same *hermeneutical* principle. "Now He said to them, 'These are My words which I spoke to you while I was still with you, that all things which are written about Me in the Law of Moses and the Prophets and the Psalms must be fulfilled.' Then He opened their minds to understand the Scriptures" (verses 44, 45). "The Law, the Prophets, and the Psalms" is the complete formula for the Jewish Scriptures that we have come to call the Old Testament. His disciples knew their Bible, but they did not understand that it was all about Jesus and the salvific act of God through Him. Jesus opened their minds! The Greek verb for "open" had been used by Luke throughout Jesus' ministry when He opened the eyes of the blind or the ears of the deaf. Now, He opens His disciples' minds! Why? To understand the Scriptures! It is possible to read the Scriptures and still have our minds closed. Our minds become open when we understand that, not just the New Testament, but all the Law of Moses, the Prophets, and the Psalms are in service to the good news of Jesus Christ.

On one of my favorite book covers, F. F. Bruce's *The New Testament Development of Old Testament Themes,* the author makes the point that the whole Bible is about the redemption achieved through Jesus:

> **"In Jesus** *the promise is confirmed, the covenant is renewed, the prophecies are fulfilled,*
> *the law is vindicated, salvation is brought near, sacred history has reached its climax,*
> *the perfect sacrifice has been offered and accepted,*
> *the great priest over the household of God has taken his seat at God's right hand,*
> *the Prophet like Moses has been raised up, the Son of David reigns,*
> *the kingdom of God has been inaugurated,*
> *the Son of Man has received dominion from the Ancient of Days,*
> *the Servant of the Lord, having been smitten to death for his people's transgressions and borne the sins of many, has accomplished the divine purpose,*
> *has seen light after the travail of his soul and is now exalted and extolled and made very high."*

Let's respond to God's amazing promise

God is more than faithful to His promises. At the cross, He fulfilled His *amazing* promise to crush the serpent's head (Genesis 3:15), and He is coming back to reclaim His children, so that we may once again live with Him, this time for eternity. In the space provided below, write down at least ten memorable events in your life, in which you believe God fulfilled His promises.

1.
2.
3.
4.
5.
6.
7.
8.
9.
10.

"The Lord is my **strength** and **song**, and He has become my **salvation**; this is my God, and I will **praise** Him." "In Your **lovingkindness** You have **led** the people whom You have **redeemed**" (Exodus 15:2, 13; emphasis added).

A loving parent does not give up, and neither does God. He announced that this was not the end, that even if He had to die for His children, He would not give up! Even though they would be separated temporarily because the humans were now mortal and had lost the *paradeisos,* God would take their death upon Himself, so that they could be together again—forever. He simply refused to go through eternity without His people.

Oh, my soul, praise His name! It is true! His love never ends!

Do you believe and accept God's amazing promise to save you? Do you accept the plan of redemption that God designed through Jesus' death as your ONLY HOPE? Take a moment to write a prayer of thanksgiving and acceptance of the AMAZING GRACE of God towards you:

Amazing Kinship

Lesson 4

Read Leviticus 25:1–13, 23–25, 47–49, 54, 55. As you read the biblical narrative, highlight words or phrases that catch your attention.

Let's study

One of the most intriguing themes running through Scripture is the one commonly referred to as "kinsman-redeemer." When someone was in distress and in need of being rescued, his or her closest relative could legally step in. If a man could no longer support himself, he could give up his property or inheritance; and if that wasn't enough, he could sell himself as a slave to pay his debt. What a terrible situation! But wait! There was a light at the end of the tunnel! The nearest kinsman or closest relative could act on the victim's behalf; he could purchase the property or land and restore it to its original owner or pay the ransom for the enslaved relative to be set free. The *closest of kin* claimed responsibility for the relative in distress. Can you imagine being that destitute and lost, and then you hear the news about your kinsman-redeemer on his way to rescue you?

The word in Hebrew for "kinsman-redeemer" is *go'el*. The *go'el* had many roles regarding the destitute relative. Leviticus 25 is one of the chapters to explain in detail some of the laws of redemption. I will highlight four of the *go'el* roles that inform our study, with a special emphasis on the first two.

1. To redeem property that was given up by a poor relative.

"If a fellow countryman of yours becomes so poor he has to sell part of his property, then his nearest kinsman [*go'el*] is to come and buy back what his relative has sold" (Leviticus 25:25). For further information, please see Leviticus 25:25–34.

2. To redeem a relative who had sold himself into slavery.

"Now if . . . a countryman of yours becomes so poor with regard to him as to sell himself to a stranger who is sojourning with you, or to the descendants of a stranger's family, then he shall have redemption right after he has been sold. One of his brothers may redeem him, . . . or one of his blood relatives from his family may redeem him" (Leviticus 25:47–49). For further study, see Leviticus 25:47–54.

3. To avenge the blood of a murdered relative.

The *go'el haddam* was the "avenger of blood." The murderer, then, would only be safe in any of the cities of refuge (see Numbers 35:12, 19–28; Deuteronomy 19:6, 12; Joshua 20:2, 3).

4. To appear in a lawsuit as a helper for a relative.

The *go'el* would make sure that justice was done (see Proverbs 23:11; Jeremiah 50:34; Psalm 119:154).

Can you imagine a person in slavery, destitute, without property, or in a lawsuit? Can you imagine the helplessness and the hopelessness the person experienced? But can you visualize the happiness and relief the same person started to feel when he or she saw the *go'el*?

The *go'el* was the redeemer, the person who looked after your safety and did whatever was necessary to take your shame away and bring you back to freedom. Your closest of kin was your hope and safety. If a person had no *go'el* and lost everything, he or she still had ONE HOPE. Yahweh, the Lord, would be his or her ultimate *Go'el,* who would step in during the year of jubilee.

And this is where it gets really good!

When God created us in *His image,* He pledged Himself to a *rescue plan* because He was our *"closest of Kin."*

He is our *Go'el.* He obligated Himself to become our Rescuer!

Fill in the blanks with your own name:
"But now, thus says the LORD, your Creator, O _____,
And He who formed you, O _____,
'Do not fear, for I have redeemed [*Go'el*-ed] you;
I have called you by name; you are Mine!' " (Isaiah 43:1).

Let's understand

Go'el, Creation, and Redemption: As a parent pledges himself or herself to rescue his or her own child when necessary, so does God. The concepts of creation and redemption were linked together from the very beginning, because God created us in His *image,* and therefore became our *closest of kin,* our *Kinsman-Redeemer.* What a fantastic and surprising concept!

Go'el is used in the Scriptures as a descriptive name for God, usually translated as Redeemer in our English Bibles. It highlights His mighty acts of redemption on behalf of His people (see Exodus 6:6; 15:13). God constantly reminds us that He is our Kinsman-Redeemer, our *Go'el,* especially in the book of Isaiah. I am particularly touched when He reminds me to "fear not" because He has acted as our *Go'el* (see Isaiah 43:1).

What would you do for your children if they were in trouble? Do you think God feels the same way about you?

Go'el, Jubilee, and Liberty: "It is clear that the close family members are obligated to act as next of kin for another member of the family. . . . If a debtor-slave has not been 'redeemed' by any of the ways provided for him to gain his freedom, he 'goes out' in the year of Jubilee. . . . This language means that the release at the year of Jubilee possesses the same quality as the exodus from Egypt. Each Jubilee, Yahweh acts again as Israel's great Redeemer" (Hartley, *Leviticus,* p. 442).

This, the Jubilee, was the favorable year of the Lord, when once every fifty years, seven times seven years (forty-nine), all slaves were to be set free, all debts were canceled, and all property returned to the original owners. If someone had a kinsman-redeemer (*go'el*), this blessed liberty could happen anytime, if and when the person's closest kin paid the ransom. But, just in case they didn't, the heavenly Kinsman-Redeemer, Yahweh (the LORD), would step in for everyone once every seven times seven years. On the Day of Atonement, the ram's horn would sound (see Leviticus 25:8–10), and everyone and everything would be set free (seven has always been the number for redemption and freedom in the Jewish Scriptures).

When the United States of America was founded, the dream was that this would be the "land of the free." That *everyone* would have freedom and liberty in this newfound land. As a reminder of this fact, the Liberty Bell bears the engraving: LEV. XXV:X. This verse reads: "Proclaim a release [or liberty] through the land to all its inhabitants" (Leviticus 25:10). That's why it is called the LIBERTY BELL!

God was very specific about the laws of redemption and the Jubilee. Why did He want us to know that He is the One who desires and secures our liberty?

Go'el, Sabbath, and Redemption of Property: "In the OT the idea of redemption is closely associated with the laws and customs of the Israelite people. . . . According to the theocratic arrangement in Israel, the land belonged to God and the Israelite families only possessed the right to use the fruit of the land. . . . If a family forfeited this use because its parcel of land had to be sold or because there was no heir, the parcel was returned to the family at the year of jubilee, which came every fifty years (Lev 25:8-17). Prior to this year the nearest kinsman had the right and the responsibility to redeem the property, i.e., to liquidate the debt so that the property might be restored to its original owner (25:23-28)" (*Zondervan Pictorial Encyclopedia of the Bible,* s.v. "Redeemer, Redemption").

"Technically, all land in Israel which had been sold reverted to the original family during the Jubilee year. Leviticus 25:25-28 provides that the person himself or his next of kin may buy the land back before the Jubilee, however" (*Zondervan Pictorial Encyclopedia of the Bible,* s.v. "Redemption of Land").

Therefore, in an amazing development of concepts not only the Sabbath day (see Exodus 20:11 and Deuteronomy 5:15) but also the sabbath year, the Day of Atonement, and the year of Jubilee would be constant celebrations of remembrance of redemption. *The Creator is also the Redeemer; the captives **and** their property (the land) were set free by Yahweh, the Lord, the ultimate Go'el.*

Let's reflect

It was a sunny afternoon and my mother and I were really enjoying ourselves. We were in La Pampa, Argentina, in a little town where my parents were conducting an evangelistic series. My dad was an evangelist, and the three of us used to move to a new location every six months.

On that sunny afternoon, I was four years old and my mother had decided to take me for a ride.

We lived in a very small mud house. There was not much for me to do at home, so my mother borrowed a bicycle to take me for a fun sightseeing ride. I was so excited! I was not old enough to ride this bike myself, so I settled in a small seat behind my mother. She was the one in charge, pedaling and steering on our tour. I was the one enjoying it in the back. So we began. We had been going for quite a while and were now far away from the town, enjoying the never-ending wheat fields. At one point, on a particularly bumpy part of the road, I started to slide sideways off the bike seat. My mother advised me to straighten up and to hold on firmly, so I wouldn't fall. And I did. And then it happened.

I started crying with utter desperation, and my mom couldn't understand why. She stopped the bike and asked me why I was crying. . . . What was happening? She couldn't see anything wrong, but I kept pointing to my feet. I had socks that covered my legs almost up to my knees, and my mom decided she had to take my socks off to find out what was going on. So she did. And then she saw it! The flesh at the bottom of my foot came off along with the sock, and she could see a white bone where my heel and my foot used to be. As I had tried to straighten up on the seat, I had accidentally stuck my foot in the moving wheel, which had badly injured my foot.

Well, my mother didn't have to think about it twice. With energy and strength that seemed to come directly from Above, my mom sat me on the main seat of the bicycle and took hold of the handlebars and started to run to take me back to town. . . . Right outside the town, she saw an ill-equipped clinic that was designed to deal with simple ailments and minor injuries, the only medical facility the town had. We went inside, and she asked for an X-ray . . . and it turned out that I had no broken bones. It took me six months, though, to recover and get the full use of my foot back. There is a tiny little scar on my heel that reminds me of that fateful day—the day when my mom also became my rescuer, because she did for me what I couldn't do for myself.

Write a story from your own life that comes to mind in this lesson:

Why did Jesus choose to read that specific section of Isaiah, "To PROCLAIM THE FAVORABLE YEAR OF THE LORD [Jubilee]" (see Isaiah 61:1, 2, Luke 4:18, 19) when He visited the synagogue in His hometown? What did Jesus really mean when "He began to say to them, 'Today this Scripture has been fulfilled in your hearing' " (Luke 4:21)?

Read these words of Scripture and reflect on how they set you free:

> *Jesus said:*
> *"The Spirit of the Lord GOD is upon me, because the LORD has anointed me*
> *to bring good news to the afflicted;*
> *He has sent me to bind up the brokenhearted,*
> *to proclaim liberty to captives and freedom to prisoners;*
> *to proclaim the favorable year of the LORD"* (Isaiah 61:1, 2).

Let's comprehend Jesus in Scripture

Jesus would be the One to become flesh, become our Brother, and redeem us without money (see Isaiah 52:3). He redeemed us with His blood; He came to die. That was the purpose—to pay the ransom because He is our *Go'el*. Jesus Himself stated that this was the purpose of His death, and in His explanation, we find a word usually associated with the *go'el* and the payment that was offered for the enslaved relative:

"For even the Son of Man did not come to be served, but to serve, and to give His life a *ransom for many*" (Mark 10:45; emphasis added).

"The ransom metaphor sums up the purpose for which Jesus gave his life

Amazing *Kinship*

and defines the complete expression of his service. The prevailing notion behind the metaphor is that of deliverance by purchase, whether a prisoner of war, a slave, or a forfeited life is the object to be delivered. Because the idea of equivalence, or substitution, was proper to the concept of a ransom, it became an integral element in the vocabulary of redemption in the OT. It speaks of a liberation which connotes a servitude or an imprisonment from which man cannot free himself. In the context of verse 45a, with its reference to the service of the Son of Man, it is appropriate to find an allusion to the Servant of the Lord in Isa. 53, who vicariously and voluntarily suffered and gave his life for the sins of others. The specific thought underlying the reference to the ransom is expressed in Isa. 53:10 which speaks of 'making his life an offering for sin.' Jesus, as the messianic Servant, offers himself as a guilt-offering (Lev. 5:14-6:7; 7:1-7; Num. 5:5-8) in compensation for the sins of the people. The release affected by this offering overcomes man's alienation from God, his subjection to death and his bondage to sin. Jesus' service is offered to God to release men from their indebtedness to God.

"The thought of substitution is reinforced by the qualifying phrase 'a ransom *for the many.*' The Son of Man takes *the place* of the many and there happens to him what would have happened to them. . . . The many had forfeited their lives, and what Jesus gives in their place is his life. In his death, Jesus pays the price that sets men free" (Lane, *The Gospel of Mark,* p. 384).

Now, let's read this verse again, but this time fill in the blank with your name:

"Even the Son of Man did not come to be served, but to serve, and to give His life a ransom for _____" (Mark 10:45; paraphrased).

Jesus redeemed us, and He also redeemed our land. That's why the new earth will be right here; we will be back to where we started in Genesis 1! Take a moment to read the last chapter of the Bible, Revelation 22.

Yes! Jesus fulfills all the roles of the *go'el.* Praise God for our Kinsman-Redeemer!

Let's respond to God's amazing kinship

Write a letter to God. Tell Him about your inability to save yourself and that you want to trust in His ability to rescue you because He is your *closest kin.* Tell Him about the things you have lost, which you believe He can redeem for you. Add your thanksgiving for His faithfulness in rescuing you for eternal life. And write to Him about your amazement at this outrageous news: that He is your closest kin. He is not only your God, not just your Savior, but your Kinsman-Redeemer!

"You, O Lord, are our Father, our Redeemer [*Go'el*] from of old is Your name" (Isaiah 63:16).

"I know that my Redeemer lives!" (Job 19:25).

I believe with all my heart that the topic of Jesus as our Kinsman-Redeemer is one of the most amazing topics in the whole Bible! As a matter of fact, it runs through the Bible as a golden thread, from Genesis to Revelation, creating the "mystery of redemption."

You are not destitute, and you are not enslaved. Even though you were kidnapped, your Rescuer stepped in. In the moment you accept your *Go'el* and what He has done for you, you are free!

"If the Son makes you free, you will be free indeed" (John 8:36)!

Do you believe and accept God's amazing kinship? Do you understand that your Creator-Redeemer has done everything that was necessary to save you and set you free? Take a moment to write a statement of acceptance of the costly ransom Jesus paid for you!

Amazing *Kinship*

Amazing Faithfulness

Lesson 5

Read Ruth 1:1–6, 8, 16–21; 2:1–3, 19, 20; 3:6–11. As you read the biblical narrative, highlight words or phrases that catch your attention.

What was the meaning of the request: "Spread your covering over your maid, for you are a close relative"?

_____

_____

Let's study

The biblical narrative brings us to one of the most fascinating themes in the Scriptures, that we started to study in our previous lesson: the *go'el*. I truly believe that once we understand this concept, present from Genesis to Revelation, we will start to comprehend the plan of salvation. *Go'el* is a Hebrew word meaning "kinsman-redeemer." The closest kin could do several things for his beloved relative that no one else could do. For example, the *go'el* could redeem a relative who had sold himself into slavery (Leviticus 25:47–54). He could set him or her free! Also, the *go'el* could redeem property that was given up by a poor relative (Leviticus 25:25–34). *And the go'el was the one who would marry the widow of a close relative who had died without descendants in order to provide for the widow and to ensure that the family lineage would continue, thus removing shame from the kin* (Deuteronomy 25:5, 6). The book of Ruth is written with this concept in mind. (Take a moment to read it; it is a fascinating love story!) When Naomi and Ruth became widows and came back to Bethlehem as two destitute women, they discovered that Boaz was their *go'el* (Ruth 2:20), and they rejoiced. Eventually, Ruth asked him to take her under his protection and provision: "I am Ruth your maid. So spread your covering over your maid, for you are a close relative [*go'el*]" (Ruth 3:9). He did, and Ruth's shame was taken away. He became her redeemer.

Well . . . here it is: When God created us in His image, He pledged Himself to a rescue plan because He was our closest kin. He is our *Go'el*, and we are His beloved.

This word becomes a descriptive name for God in the Scriptures, usually translated "Redeemer" in our Bibles (see Isaiah 63:16). When Jesus became flesh, He fulfilled all the roles of the *Go'el*, giving His life for our ransom, redeeming us with His blood, not with money (read Mark 10:45; Isaiah 52:3), as well as redeeming our land.

This is the most amazing theme running throughout the Scriptures. It explains that when we trust in the ransom paid by our *Go'el*, we can live with the assurance of eternal life. "I know that my Redeemer lives!" (Job 19:25). Oh, my dear Beloved, spread Your covering over me . . . and take my shame away.

Fill in the blanks with your own name:
"Then the women said to _____,
'Blessed is the LORD who has not left you [_____]
without a redeemer today' " (Ruth 4:14).

What does this mean to you?

Let's understand

Judah, Tamar, Ruth, and David:
The concept of the kinsman-redeemer as the one responsible to continue the kin's line runs throughout Scripture. There is a story recorded in Genesis 38 that is difficult for us to understand until we come to study this role of the *go'el*. Please pause for a moment and read Genesis 38. Interestingly enough, this story was linked eventually with Ruth, David, and Jesus in the biblical narrative.

"True to her word she [Tamar] had kept herself for marriage to Shelah, but Judah had failed to keep his promise to her. To fulfill her responsibility of having a child for her deceased husband Er, Tamar humbled herself in order to hold Judah accountable for failing to keep his word. . . . As a result, a Canaanite woman held Judah, a male Israelite, accountable to the standards that protected the continuance of the line of his eldest son. In God's providence her line led to the birth of David (Ruth 4:12, 18-22; Matt. 1:3-6). Thus both Judah and Tamar were vindicated: Tamar by reason of Judah's concession and her giving birth to twins, and Judah by admitting that Tamar had acted more righteously than he had. . . . The outcome was joyous. Tamar gave birth to twin boys" (Hartley, *Genesis,* p. 318).

God took this role of the closest of kin very seriously. Judah wasn't acting as a faithful redeemer, but Tamar kept him accountable. How did God show us His faithfulness to the covenant? Why do you think Tamar and Ruth are included in Jesus' genealogy? (See Matthew 1:3, 5.)

God as Husband/Bridegroom: How could God demonstrate the magnitude and scope of His love for us? How could He communicate the depth, width, and strength of His love for a fallen race, when the noblest values and displays of human feeling don't even come close to expressing it? Well, He decided to use the love of a husband for his wife and of parents for their child—the two deepest bonds of love that exist on this earth—to give us a glimpse of His love for us. These two metaphors are used throughout the Bible to unveil the passion of God, who loved us more than Himself and ultimately gave up His life for His people who had rejected Him.

Therefore, we find entire books in the Bible that use the husband/beloved metaphor to teach us of God's passion for us. Perhaps two of the most evident are Hosea and Song of Solomon. Consider this passage from Hosea, as God speaks of the unfaithful Israel:

> *"Therefore, behold, I will allure her,*
> *bring her into the wilderness and speak kindly to her.*
> *Then I will give her her vineyards from there,*
> *and the valley of Achor as a door of hope.*
> *And she will sing there as in the days of her youth. . . .*
> *I will betroth you to Me forever; yes, I will betroth you to Me in righteousness*
> *and in justice, in lovingkindness and in compassion, and I will betroth you to*
> *Me in faithfulness. Then you will know the* Lord*"* (Hosea 2:14, 15, 19, 20).

"These two verses form a unit [Hosea 2:19, 20]. . . . As Yahweh addresses his beloved directly, the metaphor shifts to marriage betrothal, bringing full circle the allegorical theme begun in 2:4. The emphasis is now not merely reconciliation but restoration. . . . The betrothal metaphor is expressed dramatically via the decisive threefold repetition of the verb ראל 'to betroth' in the first person common singular form" (Stuart, *Hosea-Jonah*, p. 59).

The Wedding Feast: God is a faithful Redeemer. The second coming of Christ is portrayed as the marriage of the Lamb (see Revelation 19:7–16). "At this point [Rev. 19:7-8], the song of the redeemed turns into a call for rejoicing at the wedding of the Lamb. . . . The much-awaited reunion of Christ with his bride—the church—at the Second Coming is expressed in terms of 'the wedding of the Lamb.' . . . This joining of Christ with the people whom he has purchased on the cross is the focus of the entire book of Revelation. Everything in the book moves toward that climactic triumph" (Stefanovic, *Revelation of Jesus Christ,* pp. 544, 545).

In order to have assurance of salvation through the blood of Jesus, why is it important to understand God's faithfulness to us, His bride?

Let's reflect

"He did what any husband would have done for his wife," reported an online news service recounting an emotional event that took place on January 13, 2012, as the *Costa Concordia* cruise ship was sinking off the west coast of Italy. When Francis Servel and his wife Nicole realized that the ship was going down, and the lifeboats were virtually impossible to lower, they decided to jump into the water. However, there were not enough life jackets available on the cruise liner; they only had one between the two of them. Yet Francis was a strong swimmer; he handed the life jacket to his wife and said, "Swim ahead, darling, I'll survive." She never saw him again.

The whole world was stunned when the luxury cruise ship, carrying more than four thousand passengers and crew, went down in a terrible tragedy that left many dead or injured and hundreds emotionally scarred for life. But it is in the midst of such crisis that real love reveals its true colors. Self-sacrificing love is being willing to give up one's life for that of another. Francis gave his life so that his wife of forty years could live. "I owe my life to my husband," said the now heartbroken Mrs. Servel. And she does. It is only real love that makes the ultimate sacrifice. When disaster strikes, instances of people giving their lives for their loved ones remind us that the human heart still carries the image of its Creator deep within.

How could God demonstrate the magnitude and scope of His love for us? How could He communicate the depth, width, and strength of His love for a fallen race, when the noblest values and display of feelings of humans don't even come close to expressing it? Well, He decided to use the love of a husband for his wife and a parent for his or her child, the two deepest bonds of love that exist on this earth, to give us a glimpse of His love for us. These two metaphors are used throughout the Bible to unveil the passion of a God who loved us more than Himself, and ultimately gave up His life for His people who had rejected Him.

In this chapter we will marvel at God's plan to save His people with the passion of a lover who willingly surrenders His own life for His beloved bride. The words keep ringing in my ears as if Jesus were saying them to me: "Go ahead, darling, I'll catch up," and He went to the cross and died in my place, giving me His own life jacket, that I may now have the assurance of eternal life.

Write a story from your daily life, that comes to mind in this session:

The pivotal point in the story of Naomi and Ruth comes when they realize that Boaz is their kinsman-redeemer (Ruth 2:20). What is the pivotal point in your life?

Explain the concept of your sins "being covered" as opposed to "covering your sins." (See Psalm 32:1–5 and Romans 4:1–8.)

Read the end of the story in Ruth 4:13–22. How would you summarize this redemption story? How does it relate to you?

Will you join us for this wedding feast? Repeat these words of Scripture aloud:

> *"Let us rejoice and be glad and give the glory to Him,*
> *for the marriage of the Lamb has come*
> *and His bride has made herself ready"* (Revelation 19:7).

Let's Understand Jesus in the Scriptures

Isaiah 53 has been called the "proto gospel," the first clarification that Jesus would die in our place. A striking sentence in verse 10 reminds us of the role of the *Go'el* in preserving the offspring in the covenantal line: "He will see His offspring." In His death and resurrection, Jesus is fulfilling the roles of the *Go'el*. God will now have descendants from a race that was mortal and therefore dead.

Commenting on Isaiah 53:10, Oswalt observes: "The terms that are typically used of a person favored by God are applied to him: he will see his descendants . . . he will live a long life . . . , and he will accomplish God's purposes for his life. What has made the difference? One thing only. If people will accept him as a guilt offering in their place. When that takes place, his life, far from being futile, will be the most fruitful life ever lived. Far from being childless, he will have children in every race on the earth. He will be able to say as Christ did on the night before he was crucified, 'I glorified you on earth by finishing the work that you gave me to do' (John 17:4). This point must be underlined because it is at the center of the meaning of the entire poem. . . . It is the result of one thing only: his becoming a sacrificial offering. When he does that, the entire process comes to fruition" (Oswalt, *The Book of Isaiah, Chapters 40–66,* p. 402).

It is in the context of Isaiah 53 that Jesus explains His mission in Mark 10:45. This is the climactic verse in the Gospel of Mark: "For even the Son of Man did not come to be served, but to serve, and to give His life a ransom for many." Yes! Jesus was the Suffering Servant described in the Jewish Scriptures.

(Take a moment to read Isaiah 53 and Psalm 22.) *"But the LORD was pleased to crush Him, putting Him to grief; if He would render Himself as a guilt offering, He will see His offspring, He will prolong His days, and the good pleasure of the LORD will prosper in His hand. As a result of the anguish of His soul, He will see it and be satisfied; by His knowledge the Righteous One, My Servant, will justify the many, as He will bear their iniquities. Therefore, I will allot Him a portion with the great, and He will divide the booty with the strong; because He poured out Himself to death, and was numbered with the transgressors; yet He Himself bore the sin of many, and interceded for the transgressors"* (Isaiah 53:10–12).

He would give His life as a ransom for us! The word *many* (Isaiah 53:12; Mark 10:45) is used to describe the outcome: one death would give life to many. The substitutionary death of Christ in the place of humankind, in other words "One for many," became a core doctrine in the first-century church: "For as through the one man's disobedience the many were made sinners, even so through the obedience of the One the many will be made righteous" (Romans 5:19). Through Adam we became mortals, with no possibility of offspring for God. But through Jesus we have life! I pray that the Holy Spirit may open our minds and "connect the dots" in the Bible for us, that we may rejoice about such a magnificent redemption and live with the joy of our salvation.

Soon it will be over . . . He is coming back for us . . . and I can't wait to hear these words from my Beloved: *"My beloved spoke and said to me, 'Arise, my darling, my beautiful one, come with me. See! The winter is past; the rains are over and gone. Flowers appear on the earth; the season of singing has come' "* (Song of Solomon 2:10–12, NIV). As I write, I am about to start crying . . . I can't wait for that day!

Let's respond to God's amazing faithfulness

Imagine the coming of Jesus. The time has finally arrived and your Beloved is coming for you! He has paid your price, and now He is coming back to take you home! He is eager to embrace you, and He ends the Bible reminding you of that very fact in very passionate words: "Yes, I am coming quickly" (Revelation 22:20)!

The coming of Christ is described in breathtaking terms, and we will devote an entire lesson to this topic in the future. But for now, imagine this flamboyant scene:

> *"And I saw heaven opened, and behold, a white horse, and He who sat on it is called Faithful and True, and in righteousness He judges and wages war.*
> *His eyes are a flame of fire, and on His head are many diadems;*
> *And He has a name written on Him which no one knows except Himself.*
> *He is clothed with a robe dipped in blood, and His name is called the Word of God. . . .*
> *And on His robe and on His thigh He has a name written,*
> *'KING OF KINGS, AND LORD OF LORDS' "* (Revelation 19:11–16).

I am amazed at the description of His robe. It is dipped in blood! That was the very high price my Beloved paid for my redemption! Take a few moments to list the parts of this description that take your breath away and explain why.

God gave us His life jacket, died in our place, and took our shame away! That's God's *amazing* faithfulness! At that moment the assurance given in Genesis 3:15 became a reality and now our *Go'el* is coming back for His bride. Will you join us for this marriage feast? "Let us rejoice and be glad and give the glory to Him, for the marriage of the Lamb has come and His bride has made herself ready" (Revelation 19:7). Our *Go'el,* who gave us His life jacket, who died in our place and was resurrected, is now coming back. I can't wait for that hug . . . after all these years!

Love never ends . . . and, Yes! our Beloved is coming back to take us home. REJOICE!

Do you believe and accept God's amazing faithfulness towards you? Do you believe that Jesus is coming back to take us, His bride, to live with Him forever? Take a moment to write a joyful acceptance of the gift of eternal life that your Beloved purchased for you.

Amazing Rescue

Lesson 6

Read Matthew 27:32–54. As you read the biblical narrative, highlight words or phrases that catch your attention.

What is the significance of verse 52 being placed in the Crucifixion narrative?

Let's study

We now arrive at a very solemn and amazing section: Jesus' crucifixion and resurrection, and why He died to accomplish the *amazing* rescue. In this lesson, we will primarily concentrate first on Matthew, then on Mark.

Imagine yourself as a first-century Jew. You have been expecting the coming of a Davidic ruler who would take control and establish his kingdom. Then Jesus comes, and He seems to be THE ONE! Then He dies. How could a Jewish follower of Jesus come to understand that His death was an atoning sacrifice for sin? There are three main obstacles in the Jewish mind that would complicate matters: (1) human sacrifices were not allowed by the God of Israel, as they were pagan practices (Deuteronomy 12:31); (2) one person was not allowed to die in place of another (Deuteronomy 24:16); and (3) death by crucifixion was considered a curse (Deuteronomy 21:22, 23).

Somehow, Jesus would have to interpret His death for them in a way that they could understand. The Gospels propose that Jesus interpreted His death in light of the Jewish Scriptures by using phrases and terms that would explain His death as a salvific sacrifice.

These are the four most prominent ways in which Jesus interpreted His death in light of the Jewish Scriptures in the book of Matthew:

1. *As the vicarious suffering of the Servant of Yahweh.* To understand this explanation, compare Matthew 20:28 with Isaiah 53.

2. *As a covenant sacrifice.* To understand this interpretation, read Matthew 26:27, 28 in light of the events recorded in Exodus 24:3–8.

3. *As the sacrifice of the beloved Son.* For more information, read Matthew 21:33–45 and Mark 12:1, 2 with the Old Testament story of the beloved son recorded in Genesis 22.

4. *As the suffering of the Righteous One.* This one will be our focus. Next, we are going to compare Matthew 27:33–54 and Psalm 22. It would be a good idea to read Psalm 22 now.

Matthew narrates Jesus' crucifixion using words and terms from Psalm 22. For example, consider Matthew 27:35: "And when they crucified Him, they divided up His garments among themselves by casting lots." And now, compare that with Psalm 22:18: "They divide my garments among them, and for my clothing they cast lots." Let's read a few more verses from Matthew: "And those passing by were hurling abuse at Him, wagging their heads. . . . 'He trusts in God; let God rescue Him now, if He delights in Him; for He said, "I am the Son of God" ' " (Matthew 27:39–42). Back to Psalm 22: "All who see me sneer at me; they separate with the lip, they wag the head, saying, 'Commit yourself to the LORD; let Him deliver him; let Him rescue him, because He delights in him' " (Psalm 22:7, 8). One more: "For dogs have surrounded me; a band of evildoers has encompassed me; they pierced my hands and my feet" (Psalm 22:16).

Can you believe that this psalm was written one thousand years before Jesus' death? How amazing that God would inspire David with such prophetic words! Prophecies fill me with awe! I serve a God who is sovereign. Psalm 22 is the Psalm of the Righteous Sufferer. The cry of anguish comes from one who has been faithful to God (Psalm 22:8–10). Jesus cried out: "My God, My God, why have You forsaken Me?" (Matthew 27:46), quoting Psalm 22:1. Jesus understood His death as that of a sinless victim, a righteous sufferer . . . *Oh, yes! Jesus was forsaken so that you may never be!*

Matthew points out that this occurred about the ninth hour (3:00 P.M.). This time would place Jesus' death at the time of the slaughter of the Passover lamb. No wonder other New Testament writers make a direct connection between Jesus and the Passover lamb! (See 1 Corinthians 5:7: "Christ our Passover also has been sacrificed.")

Let's understand

Replace all the first-person plural pronouns with your name:
"But *he* was pierced for _____'s [our] transgressions, *he* was crushed for _____'s [our] iniquities; the punishment that brought _____ [us] peace was on *him*, and by *his* wounds _____ is [we are] healed" (Isaiah 53:5, NIV; emphasis added).

Eternal Life Results From Jesus' Substitutionary Death:

Matthew's narrative of Jesus' death is the most dramatic of the four Gospels. He mentions that the veil of the temple was torn in two from top to bottom; and he also mentions that there was an earthquake—the earth shook and the rocks split (Matthew 27:51). Matthew can't wait to tell us that Jesus' death on the cross is, in fact, a victory! So after letting us know that there was an earthquake, he records the following event: "The tombs were opened, and many bodies of the saints who had fallen asleep were raised; and coming out of the tombs after His resurrection they entered the holy city and appeared to many" (Matthew 27:52, 53). There was a long-held expectation that when the Messianic age started, when the Davidic king started his everlasting reign, the dead would rise to life (see Isaiah 26:19; Daniel 12:2). Matthew is announcing that through Jesus' death this new age has started. Full victory has been gained over death.

When Adam and Eve sinned (Genesis 2:17; 3:19), we became mortals. Jesus' death in our place gave us eternal life again (see 2 Corinthians 5:21). Death had been conquered by Jesus' death on our behalf. This is when we start realizing the full and deeper meaning of the promise in Genesis 3:15.

"Although these raisings of the dead saints, like those in the Old Testament, do not mean that they will not die again, they prefigure Judaism's anticipated final resurrection, when the dead will be raised never to die again" (Keener, *The IVP Bible Background Commentary: New Testament*, p. 128). This foreshadowing also applies to the new Israel, Christ's church. "Matthew seems to be saying that with the death of Jesus history has begun its final rush to the eschatological denouement. That which happens now in miniature is an intimation, an anticipation, of what is due to happen on a grand, even a cosmic, scale" (Nolland, *The Gospel of Matthew*, p. 1214). When you believe in Jesus' death, what exactly guarantees your eternal life?

Jesus' Resurrection and Authority:

I absolutely love the language Matthew uses for the Resurrection morning. Another earthquake: "For an angel of the Lord descended from heaven and came and rolled away the stone and sat upon it" (Matthew 28:2). Sat on it! This is so like Matthew! It is "sitting on the throne" type of language, except that this time the angel sat on the stone of Jesus' tomb. Death has been conquered! Think about it for a moment. Imagine the angel sitting on the stone that was placed in front of Jesus' tomb. The angel sat on it—sat on it! As if saying: "Any questions, anyone?"

The Gospel of Matthew ends with an authoritative statement of Jesus before the Great Commission: "All authority has been given to Me in heaven and on earth" (Matthew 28:18). "[This statement] echoes Dan 7:14, 'To him was given dominion and glory and kingship, that all peoples, nations, and languages should serve him,' a kingship which is to be everlasting and indestructible; there will be further echoes of Dan 7:14 in the mission to 'all the nations' (v. 19), and in Jesus' powerful presence until 'the end of the age' (v. 20)" (France, *The Gospel of Matthew*, p. 1112).

The fact that the tomb was *empty* (see Matthew 28:6; Luke 24:1–3) is the core theological proclamation regarding the Resurrection for the Christian church until today. This was not some kind of spiritual resurrection with the body still in the tomb. No! This was not just the resurrection of Christ's divinity, with His humanity remaining in death. No! Jesus was resurrected, body and soul. THE TOMB IS EMPTY! He lives! And "all authority" has been given to Him!

Jesus possesses complete authority, in heaven and on earth. What difference does this statement make for you as you face situations out of your control?

New Way to God's Presence: The sacrificial system foreshadowed the Redeemer. Once a year, on the Day of Atonement (see Leviticus 16), the high priest would enter the veil to the Most Holy Place where, through the sprinkling of blood, the sins of the people were atoned. When Jesus died, this veil was torn: "And behold, the veil of the temple was torn in two from top to bottom" (Matthew 27:51). "The curtain of the temple is torn, confirming that a new way to God's presence has been opened up through Jesus' death" (Strauss, *Four Portraits, One Jesus,* p. 238).

This amazing truth will be further explained in the book of Hebrews: "Therefore, brethren, since we have confidence to enter the holy place by the blood of Jesus, by a new and living way which He inaugurated for us through the veil, that is, His flesh, and since we have a great priest over the house of God, let us draw near with a sincere heart in full assurance of faith" (Hebrews 10:19–22). Yes! In *full assurance of faith* through His blood. That's the *new and amazing way*.

Let's reflect

We had spent the whole day at the church, and this was the last meeting of the afternoon. My dad was preaching, and my mom was taking care of me, a six-month-old baby at the time. My mother was a nurturing mom, affable and caring, but shy in public, and her usual role was to sit quietly in church next to me as I slept peacefully. However, everything suddenly changed! Unexpectedly, a strange man, whom some members had seen around the church before, came running into the sanctuary, heading straight for the place where my mom and I sat, snatched me from the seat, and took off before anybody realized what had happened. JUST LIKE THAT!

But my mother, as quiet, soft, and shy as she usually was, at this moment turned into a whole different person! She started running after the kidnapper. The man kept running and my mother after him. Finally, he got to his pickup truck, and my mother jumped into the truck on the passenger side. He said, "Come with me, and I will explain everything." But my mother did not need his invitation; she was determined to be where I was, no matter what. He drove like a madman, as if the world was on fire. Finally, they got to a building that my mother did not recognize. He got out of the truck and ran upstairs holding me, with my mother in tow. When he finally entered a well-furnished suite, my mother realized that this was a radio station. Here the "kidnapper" was greeted by a radio announcer on air: "CONGRATULATIONS TO THE FIRST PERSON WHO BROUGHT TO OUR STATION A BABY UNDER TWELVE MONTHS OLD!"

Well, it turned out that this was a game that they often used to play on the radio back then, and the first person to show up with the requested object (in this case, a baby under one year) won a pretty sizable prize. Today, we cannot even imagine such a game being played by any town's radio station—and with impunity at that. However, in those days, it obviously did not seem like such a big deal. Whatever the case may be, my mother would never let me go and would risk her life in the process if she had to. All of this happened just because, instinctively from the very beginning, my mother had made a covenant with me that she would take care of me, no matter what! Wherever I went, she would go; whatever danger should threaten me, she would be my protector and my shield. Her self-sacrificing and nurturing spirit was not a weakness but her greatest strength instead. Such a response from a parent to a possible kidnapper is a perfect example of God's love and zeal to protect and rescue His own children.

Write a story from your daily life that comes to mind in this session:

Read these verses and reflect on each Gospel writer's unique perspective on Jesus' death and resurrection:
- MATTHEW: (Read Matthew 27:50–53; 28:18–20—Notice Matthew's beginning and end with the Presence of GOD! 1:23; 28:20.) When describing Jesus' death, why is Matthew's triumphant and victorious language important for my daily life? Do I need to be reminded today that "the angel sat on the stone"?
- LUKE: (Read the dialogue between Jesus and the thief on the cross [Luke 23:33–43] and His explanation on the road to Emmaus that ALL the Scriptures [Law, Psalms, and Prophets] are about Him [Luke 24:19–27, 44–45].) Why is it important to know that Jesus promised Paradise to this undeserving man? Notice Luke begins and ends with GREAT (Greek: *mega*) JOY (compare 2:10, 11 and 24:52, 53—angels and disciples).

- JOHN: (Read about Jesus being the pre-existing God [1:1] who became flesh [1:14].) John wrote with a very specific purpose: that we may BELIEVE (verb used more than ninety times in this Gospel) that Jesus is the Christ and in Him we have eternal life (read John 20:30, 31). One of His disciples first couldn't believe but then recognized Jesus as "my Lord and my God" (see John 20:26–29). Jesus then pronounced a blessing for YOU! Don't miss it! Read John 20:29.
- MARK: We will study this Gospel's perspective below.

Let's comprehend Jesus in Scripture

In this section, I want to concentrate on the way Jesus treated failing people . . . such as Peter. There is one chapter in the Gospel of Mark where we find Peter's name mentioned nine times, more than in any other chapter in this Gospel. It is one of the most meaningful times for Jesus and His disciples, and it is the moment when Jesus explains that the Passover Feast was a symbol of His death. Take a moment to read this fascinating account in Mark 14:22–31. Now they are to understand that Jesus Himself is the Passover Lamb, whose blood of the covenant is poured out as a ransom for many (1 Corinthians 5:7; Mark 10:45).

After these incredible revelations, they sing a hymn and go out to the Mount of Olives (Mark 14:26). Then Jesus makes the strangest announcement: "You will all fall away, because it is written, 'I will strike down the shepherd, and the sheep shall be scattered.' But after I have been raised, I will go ahead of you to Galilee" (Mark 14:27, 28). What kind of God is this? Who makes a covenant to give His life as a ransom for people that He knows are going to fail Him? In one of the most unbelievable juxtapositions recorded in the Bible, Jesus is saying that His blood of the covenant would be poured out, and at the same time He is saying that His own disciples would abandon Him. Then He goes on: "But after I have been raised, I will go ahead of you to Galilee" (verse 28). What? You will still want to see us? Even if we failed You? Seriously, what kind of God are You, Jesus?

And there goes Peter . . . "OK, Jesus, maybe some of the 'weaklings' among the disciples might need a Savior like that, you know, for failing people. But I am Peter, and that's not going to happen to me! No way!" The actual scriptural version is recorded in Mark 14:29, 31. But Jesus knew Peter better than Peter knew himself: "And Jesus said to him, 'Truly I say to you, that this very night, before a rooster crows twice, you yourself will deny Me three times' " (verse 30). This is how thoroughly he would deny Him. This is how complete his failure would be!

You may read Peter's terrible failure and denial in Mark 14:66–72. The account ends in a description of Peter's desperate situation: "And Peter remembered how Jesus had made the remark to him, 'Before a rooster crows twice, you will deny Me three times,' and he began to weep" (verse 72). Yes, Peter had failed Jesus . . . like many of us have. Mark doesn't mention Peter throughout the Crucifixion and Jesus' burial.

It's like he doesn't deserve to be in the picture anymore. But Mark tells us something that no other Gospel writer records on the morning of the Resurrection: "Entering the tomb, they saw a young man sitting at the right, wearing a white robe; and they were amazed. And he said to them, 'Do not be amazed; you are looking for Jesus the Nazarene, who has been crucified. He has risen; He is not here; behold, here is the place where they laid Him. But go, tell His disciples *and Peter,* "He is going ahead of you to Galilee; there you will see Him, just as He told you" ' " (Mark 16:5–7; emphasis added). Did you CATCH THAT? Did you see the **two words**? The one who had failed is called by name! Jesus didn't want Peter to think that he was excluded. His blood had covered even *his ransom,* and I have become convinced that it even covered mine.

> Fill in the blank with your name, to receive His assurance:
> "Tell His disciples and _____,
> 'He is going ahead of you . . . you will see Him, just as He told you.' "

Let's respond to God's amazing rescue

Have you ever written a song to God? Well, this is your chance. We are told that the sacrifice of Jesus to redeem humanity will be the theme of a "new song" throughout eternity:

> *"And they sang a **new song,** saying, 'Worthy are You to take the book and to break its seals; for You were slain, and purchased for God with Your blood men from every tribe and tongue and people and nation. You have made them to be a kingdom and priests to our God; and they will reign upon the earth' "* (Revelation 5:9, 10; emphasis added).

This is the story of our Creator-Redeemer and the greatest "love surprise" of all time. It amazed Adam and Eve. It amazed the deceitful serpent. It amazed the Pharisees. It amazed the disciples. It even amazed the heavenly angels. And it continues to amaze us today.

The deceiver thought that he had outsmarted God! He never expected that love would win. Perhaps humans themselves thought that they were beyond redemption! But "where sin increased, grace abounded all the more" (Romans 5:20).

> So, take a moment to praise and magnify Jesus (the Lamb of God) for rescuing you and assuring you that in Him you have eternal life.

Amazing *Rescue*

Amazing Love

Lesson 7

Read John 3:1–18 and Numbers 21:4-9. Then read the second story in John 8:2–11. As you read the biblical narratives, highlight words or phrases that catch your attention.

Let's study

Nicodemus was a Pharisee, and, as such, he carefully observed the law and held high the traditions of the elders. His name, though Greek, was used among the Jews. But he was no ordinary Jew; he was a ruler of the Jews, most likely a member of the Sanhedrin (John 7:45–52), the ruling council of the Jews. He kept the law, he taught the law, he interpreted the law—he seemed to have it all together. The diplomatic ruler opens with an impressive assertion: "Rabbi, we know that You have come from God . . . for no one can do these signs that You do unless God is with him" (verse 2). Curiously, he speaks in the plural ("*we* know"). He represents a group, a ruling group of educated and religious people.

Skipping the expected flattery, Jesus introduces His shattering comment with an emphatic, "Truly, truly, I say to you" (verse 3). In one sentence, Jesus overthrows the entire means of salvation that Nicodemus believed in. In the only passage in this Gospel that mentions the kingdom of God (verses 3 and 5), Jesus explains that whatever Nicodemus stands for is not enough for salvation. Jesus then addresses him in plural, perhaps sending a message to the group he represents or to the entire human race: "Do not be amazed that I said to you, 'You [you people] must be born again' " (verse 7). I guess many of us are startled when we realize that our law-keeping is not enough for salvation.

Then Jesus tells the snake story. You see, Nicodemus knew the history of Israel like the back of his hand. Jesus decides to explain salvation through this story found in Numbers 21:4–9. Take a moment to read it. The people of Israel are tired and impatient. They hate the food. They hate everything. God removes His protection from them in the middle of the miserable desert. Venomous snakes start biting the people, and many die. Israel repents. They ask Moses to intercede with Yahweh (the Lord) on their behalf. God comes up with seemingly the most ridiculous antidote to snakebites ever: "Make a fiery serpent, and set it on a standard [pole]; and it shall come about, that everyone who is bitten, when he looks at it, he will live" (verse 8). It is only natural to want to drink something or inject something to counteract the venom. This is how an antidote works. You get it into your system. But salvation in this case would happen when those who were bitten looked in faith to the bronze serpent. Salvation was outside their system, hanging on a pole.

It is in this narrative that the best known verse of the entire Bible is found. "As Moses lifted up the serpent in the wilderness, even so must the Son of Man be lifted up; so that whoever believes will in Him have eternal life. *For God so loved the world, that He gave His only begotten Son, that whoever believes in Him shall not perish, but have eternal life.* For God did not send the Son into the world to judge the world, but that the world might be saved through Him" (John 3:14–17; emphasis added). Why would Jesus identify Himself with a snake? Doesn't the serpent represent the devil, evil, and sin? Oh, yes! That's the beauty of the typology (symbol). "He made Him who knew no sin to be sin on our behalf, so that we might become the righteousness of God in Him" (2 Corinthians 5:21).

Let's understand

Grace, Law, and Judgment: The law of God gives us a glimpse into His character and the beauty that He intends for humanity. It is not an arbitrary set of rules but a description of the wholeness that His kingship brings about in our lives. We can truly say, with the apostle Paul, that "the Law is holy, and the commandment is holy and righteous and good" (Romans 7:12). We can summarize the role of the law in the Christian's life in three main categories:

- **The law exposes our sin:** It's like a mirror that confronts us with our sinfulness. (See James 1:22–25; Romans 3:20.)
- **The law points us to our need for a Savior:** It guides us to Christ as our only hope. (See Galatians 3:24.)
- **Love is the fulfillment of the law:** The Holy Spirit writes the spirit of the law in the heart of those who are under grace, to love God and their neighbor, which is the fulfillment of all the Law and the Prophets. (See Romans 13:8–10; Matthew 22:36–40; Jeremiah 31:31–34.)

But, unfortunately, because of our fallen nature, the law of God cannot save us, even though it is good and holy. God had to come up with a plan, *apart from the law*, to save us. This *amazing* plan is called GRACE and it was fulfilled when Jesus took our place at the cross: "But now *apart from the Law* the righteousness of God has been manifested, being witnessed by the Law and the Prophets, even the righteousness of God through faith in Jesus Christ for all those who believe; for there is no distinction; for all have sinned and fall short of the glory of God, *being justified as a gift by His grace through the redemption which is in Christ Jesus*" (Romans 3:21–24; emphasis added). This is the relationship between grace, law, and judgment. When we talk about "justified," then we already know the verdict of the judgment: we are declared "just" or "not guilty" on account of the ransom paid by Jesus, which we accept by faith (see Romans 3:25, 26). That is why those who are under grace are no longer under the judgment of the law.

Commenting on Romans 3:21–26, Moo summarizes these concepts with pristine clarity: "Paul, then, is indicating that all people fail to exhibit that 'being-like-God' for which they were created; and the present tense of the verb, in combination with Rom. 8, shows that even Christians 'fall short' of that goal until they are transformed in the last day by God. . . . Paul uses the verb 'justify' (*dikaioō*) for the first time in Romans to depict his distinctive understanding of Christian salvation. As Paul uses it in these contexts, the verb 'justify' means not 'to make righteous' (in an ethical sense) nor simply 'to treat as righteous' (though one is really not righteous), but 'to declare righteous.' No 'legal fiction,' but a legal *reality* of the utmost significance, 'to be justified' means to be acquitted by God from all 'charges' that could be brought against a person because of his or her sins. This judicial verdict, for which one had to wait until the last judgment according to Jewish theology, is according to Paul rendered the moment a person believes. The act of justification is therefore properly 'eschatological,' [end time events] as the ultimate verdict regarding a person's standing with God is brought back into our present reality.

"Characteristic also of Paul's theology is his emphasis on the gift character of this justifying verdict; we are 'justified freely by his grace.' 'Grace' is one of Paul's most significant theological terms. He uses it typically not to describe a quality of God but the way in which God has acted in Christ; unconstrained by anything beyond his own will. God's justifying verdict is totally unmerited. People have done, and can do, nothing to earn it. This belief is a 'theological axiom' for Paul and is the basis for his conviction that justification can never be attained through works, or the law (cf. Rom. 4:3-5, 13-16; 11:6), but only through faith" (Moo, *The Epistle to the Romans,* pp. 226–228).

Fill in the blanks with your own name:
"For God so loved _____ that He gave His only begotten Son, that _____ [who] believes in Him shall not perish, but have eternal life" (John 3:16).

Do you take this statement at face value, or do you add any conditions to it, such as "plus," "and," "but," "if," and so on? Why or why not?

Grace and Wholeness: Read John 8:2–11. God desires a life of happiness and wholeness for His children, and His grace provides us with *"freedom from"* and *"freedom to"* opportunities: *freedom from* shame, guilt, and habits that enslave us, and *freedom to* live our lives with joy, gratitude, and purpose, for His glory and our happiness. There is no greater power for transforming our lives than the power of grace. Unlike other extrinsic motivators, grace motivates intrinsically, from within.

"In His act of pardoning this woman and encouraging her to live a better life, the character of Jesus shines forth in the beauty of perfect righteousness. While He does not palliate sin, nor lessen the sense of guilt, He seeks not to condemn, but to save. The world had for this erring woman [adulterous woman] only contempt and scorn; but Jesus speaks words of comfort and hope. The Sinless One pities the weakness of the sinner, and reaches to her a helping hand. While the hypocritical Pharisees denounce, Jesus bid her, 'Go, and sin no more.'

"Men hate the sinner, while they love the sin. Christ hates the sin, but loves the sinner. This will be the spirit of all who follow Him. Christian love is slow to censure, quick to discern penitence, ready to forgive, to encourage, to set the wanderer in the path of holiness, and to stay his feet therein" (White, *The Desire of Ages*, p. 462).

Knowing yourself "loved" by God, in spite of everything you have done or have become, is the beginning of a new life. This is why it is so important to pay attention to the order of Jesus' words, because He speaks to us in the same manner. First: "I don't condemn you." Then: "Go, sin no more." His love and grace PRECEDE our confession, repentance, and transformation.

Let's reflect

It was a beautiful sunny day, and my husband, Patrick, was walking with a friend of his to the office on a long bridge above the busy Panamericana, a high-speed freeway in the city of Buenos Aires. The wide bridge was designed for cars, but it also had a pedestrian walkway with an approximately four-feet-high metal barrier on the side of the bridge. Halfway across the bridge, they noticed a man with a distressed look on his face standing at the side of the bridge. Having noticed the unusual expression in the man's eyes, Patrick, when he arrived at the next corner, turned around to see if the man was OK. As he looked, the man was swinging one of his legs over the railing. Patrick started running back; when he got to the stranger, he had already managed to swing his other leg over the barrier and was now standing on the outer side of it, ready to jump down into the busy traffic below. Now nothing was keeping this man from jumping. And the traffic below was so fast and busy that the fall would mean a sure death.

Without one second to spare, my husband grabbed this man with both arms from behind and held him as firmly as possible. The metal barrier was between them, but it was short enough for Patrick to be able to lock his own hands around the man's chest, preventing him from jumping. The man kept screaming, "Let me go! Let me go!" But Patrick would not let him go; he kept telling him, "God loves you! God loves you!" Time froze as they wrestled—the man toward death and Patrick toward life. After a few minutes, the man realized that Patrick was not about to let him go, and he started crying, explaining that he had not been able to purchase milk for his baby girl for the last three days. He was desperate, with no money and no way out. Eventually, he made his way back to Patrick's side and, sobbing, he told him that he was a Christian but that he had become too desperate to think straight. He was helpless and hopeless. When this desperate man had lost his ability to hang in there, God held on to him with a strong grip—in this case, through Patrick's arms.

Write an instance from your daily life that comes to mind in this session:

Let's read John 8:2–11 once again. The scribes and the Pharisees used the Law of Moses to condemn this woman. Is the law opposed to grace? How do you reconcile the fact that the same God who wrote the tablets of the Law also wrote on the ground that day and did not condemn the guilty woman? (See John 8:6–11.)

Jesus announced the sentence and said that whoever is without sin should throw the first stone. Why didn't He throw the stone, since He was the ONLY ONE without sin? "Jesus said, 'I do not condemn you, either. Go. From now on sin no more'" (John 8:11). Why is the order of Jesus' words to the sinful woman so important for us today?

Repeat these words of Scripture aloud until you believe what they say:

"There is now no condemnation for those who are in Christ Jesus."
"For I am convinced that neither death, nor life, nor angels, nor principalities, nor things present, nor things to come, nor powers, nor height, nor depth, nor any other created thing, will be able to separate us from the love of God, which is in Christ Jesus our Lord" (Romans 8:1, 38, 39).

Let's comprehend Jesus in Scripture

In this section we will further explore the relationship between God's holy and perfect law and the grace we receive through Jesus Christ's sacrifice on our behalf. The charge against this woman is clear: *adultery*. It is a serious charge, even mentioned in the Ten Commandments (see Exodus 20:14; Deuteronomy 5:18). The Jewish law required witnesses in order to make such a charge; therefore, the narrative clearly states that this woman was caught "in the very act" (John 8:4). Adultery was one of the three gravest sins for Jews; they would rather die than be caught in idolatry, murder, or adultery. The scribes and the Pharisees refer to the Law of Moses: "Now in the Law Moses commanded us to stone such women; what then do You say?" (verse 5).

Two passages in the Pentateuch deal with such laws: Leviticus 20:10 and Deuteronomy 22:22–24. In Leviticus 20:10, if a man has sexual relations with the wife of a neighbor, both shall be put to death. The method is not identified. The law in Deuteronomy 22:22–24 required stoning *only* when the girl was a virgin engaged to be married. There is no mention of such being the case; neither is there a man present to receive the death penalty also; and this is not taking place at the gate of the city. There is no doubt that the scribes and the Pharisees are manipulating the law a bit. The narrative tells us that their motive is to test Jesus "so that they might have grounds for accusing Him" (verse 6). But the truth is, apart from all the excuses and manipulations of her accusers, the woman is guilty!

At this point, you can insert here your own sin for which you may be wondering if Jesus' blood can cover it: adultery, pride, stealing, murder of the body or of the soul, bad parenting, lying, self-righteousness, and so forth. I am sure you have something to put in. If you think you don't, well—read 1 John 1:10. So, now that you and I know that we are all as guilty as was the adulterous woman, we know this sentence applies to us: "All have sinned and fall short of the glory of God" (Romans 3:23). Now you are ready to experience what the adulterous woman experienced that day. Only those who understand the bad news can rejoice with the good news!

"Jesus said to her, 'Woman, where are they? Did no one condemn you?' She said, 'No one, Lord.' And Jesus said, 'I do not condemn you, either. Go. From now on sin no more' " (John 8:10, 11). You see, Jesus aborted this stoning, and, a few days later, the only One who was qualified to throw the stone did throw the stone. But He threw the stone on Himself, and in doing so He took the penalty that she deserved. That we all deserve. When Jesus was hanging on the cross, John records Him as saying, "It is finished!" (John 19:30). What was finished? All condemnation for those who believe in Jesus was finished, because the sinless Son of God took humanity's death penalty upon Himself. The entire sacrificial system of the Jewish Scriptures was pointing to this very moment. No wonder that in the first chapter of this Gospel (verse 29), Jesus is introduced as "the Lamb of God who takes away the sin of the world!" Jesus always speaks to us in the same order. First, "I do not condemn you"; then, "Go . . . sin no more." God wants us to live healthier lives for His glory and for our happiness, but He never reverses the order. He never says, "Sin no more, and then I won't condemn you." He has already paid our death penalty on the cross. If you accept that, you are not condemned; if you reject it, then you are judged guilty. "He who believes in Him is not judged; he who does not believe has been judged already, because he has not believed in the name of the only begotten Son of God" (John 3:18).

Let's respond to God's amazing love

There are many days, sometimes weeks, months, and years, when we feel condemned, guilty as charged. Sometimes, other people condemn us; sometimes, we condemn ourselves. Guilt is heavy, and it disables us by not allowing us to become who God has designed us to be. I urge you, in the name of Jesus, who aborted the stoning in the temple court, to be free today.

Let's respond to His grace. First, let's place ourselves in the middle of the temple court. Ready? This visualization might be useful to you: sit on the floor and close your eyes; imagine yourself in the center of the court. You know you are guilty. Perhaps no one else knows. Listen to the charge that you deserve to die. Now confess your sin and claim Jesus' blood on your behalf. Then listen to Jesus' response to you: "I don't condemn you; go and sin no more." This is the good news. Leave your burden at the foot of the cross. Get up from the ground, and go on to live a life for God's glory to the full potential that His Spirit enables you to.

You are now ready to move on! Write this verse (Psalm 103:12) on a nice piece of paper and tape it to your mirror, the one you use every morning:

"As far as the east is from the west,
So far has He removed our transgressions from us."

His Grace is *sufficient*! And His Love is *amazing*!

Take a moment to write your acceptance of being "justified or declared just" by faith in Jesus and your desire to live for God's glory from now on (see Ephesians 2:8–10).

Amazing Assurance

Lesson 8

Read Luke 23:33–49; 24:1–9. This is one of the most significant narratives in the Bible. As you read the biblical narrative, highlight the words or phrases that catch your attention.

Let's study

In response to a charge from the Pharisees and the scribes, Jesus tells three of the most famous parables in the Bible: the lost sheep, the lost coin, and the lost son (Luke 15). The third parable Jesus tells here is the climactic story of the lost son who requests his inheritance before his father dies, rejecting his father, his family, and his kin. (Please take a moment to read the whole parable in Luke 15:11–32.) The younger son, deciding that he knows better than anyone else how to run his life, starts on a journey that will lead to a crescendo of infamy—from his request of the inheritance to its disbursement, then to his departure, and finally to when he squanders all he has. Eventually he hits bottom, as he has nothing to eat, and hires himself to feed swine—an unthinkable job for a Jew. Then a light goes on . . . and he decides to go back to his father and ask for a job! But his father, who has been waiting for him all along, sees him when he is still afar off, runs to him, embraces him, and offers him three things that are symbolic acts of restoration: the best robe, the ring, and the sandals. He was a son again! Then the father kills the fattened calf, and they start to celebrate the "homecoming" (even though not everyone in the family is celebrating).

Just when you thought it was only a parable, Luke records a fascinating real-life dialogue that will bring the previous parable to life. It is found in Luke 23:32–43. Let's start from the beginning. Jesus is dying on the cross: "Two others also, who were criminals, were being led away to be put to death with Him. When they came to the place called The Skull, there they crucified Him and the criminals, one on the right and the other on the left" (verses 32, 33). The names of the criminals are not specified in this narrative; all we know is that both are evildoers. The Greek word for "criminal," *kakourgos,* is composed of two words: *kakos* ("evil, bad, wrong") and *ergon* ("work, deed, action"). In the most literal sense of the word, both of them are "evil-workers." They have squandered their lives and now are getting what they deserve.

And then, unexpectedly, one of the criminals turns to Jesus and utters the most outrageous and astonishing request, just like the prodigal son! "Can I come back home and have part of the inheritance?" In other words, "Jesus, remember me when You come in Your kingdom!" (verse 42).

Let's divide the request into three parts, in order to understand its deeper meaning. First of all, the *undeserving* man calls Christ by His name: *Jesus.* He did not call Him "Rabbi," or "Messiah," or "Lord"; he called Him "Jesus," a name that, by its own definition, recalls that "Yahweh saves" (*Jesus* is the Greek version of the Hebrew name *Joshua*). The name by which the criminal addresses Jesus is in itself a remembrance of salvation! (See Matthew 1:21.)

The second part of the request is, "Remember me." This type of request was usually addressed to Yahweh in the Jewish Scriptures. When Yahweh remembered somebody, it didn't mean that the person was just coming back to His mind, but it carried the blessing of His action on behalf of His people in keeping with His covenant. There are many examples of such requests to Yahweh (see Judges 16:28; 1 Samuel 1:11). So this request is not about Jesus having memories of him but about Jesus acting on his behalf.

The third part of the request, "When You come in Your kingdom," shows that this criminal had come to believe that the Crucifixion was not the end of Jesus. Furthermore, he had come to understand that beyond the cross was the kingdom and that, in fact, Christ's suffering was consistent with His kingship, not contrary to it. But . . . why would Jesus even listen to this *younger son*? Has he not caused enough shame already? What follows is the most surprising response, which is narrated only in the Gospel of Luke, the core theological theme of which is "salvation for all." We will concentrate on Jesus' answer in the following section of this lesson.

Fill in the blanks with your own name:
"Jesus, remember me, _____, when You come in Your kingdom!"
"Truly I say to you, _____ today, *with Me* you, _____, will be in Paradise" (Luke 23:42, 43, paraphrased; emphasis added).

Let's understand

Assurance, not Fear: The word *assurance* appears in the New Testament more times in the book of Hebrews than in any other place (see Hebrews 3:14; 6:11; 10:22; 11:1). "Faith is the *assurance* of things hoped for" (Hebrews 11:1; emphasis added). And this assurance is given to us because of Jesus' sacrifice on the cross and His continued intercession for us, presenting His blood on our behalf in the heavenly sanctuary. The book of Hebrews takes the Old Testament typology (symbols and foreshadows of Jesus' ministry) and explains it in light of the cross. It is the book of "better hope, better covenant, better sacrifice, and better priest." It is all about Jesus, and when the believer understands what He has achieved through His blood, there is only one reality left: *assurance*!

Therefore, whether we are discussing our salvation, our daily lives, or end-time events, *fear* is no longer part of the equation; *assurance* has taken over.

F. F. Bruce's comments on Hebrews 10:19–25 are very insightful: "The 'boldness' which believers in Christ have to enter the heavenly sanctuary through him is set in contrast with the restrictions which hedged about the privilege of symbolic entry into the presence of God in Israel's earthly sanctuary. In it not all the people could exercise this privilege, but the high priest only, as their representative; and even he could not exercise the privilege any time he chose, but at fixed times and under fixed conditions. But those who have been cleansed within, consecrated and made perfect by the sacrifice of Christ, have received a free right of access into the holy presence; and our author urges his readers to avail themselves fully of this free right. . . . The way by which they enter the presence of God is a new way, which did not exist until he opened it up and entered thereby himself. It is thus a new way; it is also a 'living way.' For in effect the ever-living Christ himself, as his people's sacrifice and priest, is the way to God. . . . Those who have experienced the inward cleansing that Christ's self-offering has effected may well be marked by sincerity of heart and 'faith's full assurance' " (Bruce, *The Epistle to the Hebrews,* pp. 249, 250, 254).

Death and Paradise: Up to the Christian Era, fear of death was common, paralyzing, and widespread. People were terrified by the very thought of death and the unknown surrounding it. When Jesus lived, died, and conquered death, He radically changed the way His followers spoke about death. No longer was it a horrifying event, but a sweet sleep instead (see John 11:11–15). The deceased are resting, awaiting the resurrection morning, when they will hear a loud Voice calling them out of their tombs and welcoming them to Paradise.

"I say unto thee today, Thou shalt be with Me in Paradise. Christ did not promise that the thief should be with Him in paradise that day. He Himself did not go that day to Paradise. He slept in the tomb, and on the morning of the resurrection He said, 'I am not yet ascended to My Father.' John 20:17. But on the day of the crucifixion, the day of apparent defeat and darkness, the promise was given. 'Today' while dying upon the cross as a malefactor, Christ assures the poor sinner, Thou shalt be with Me in Paradise" (White, *The Desire of Ages,* p. 751).

"The criminal . . . is the first to recognize that Jesus' death is not a contradiction of his messiahship, his role as Savior; he is the first to recognize that Jesus' crucifixion is a precursor to his enthronement . . . and that he anticipates in his request Jesus' kingly rule. 'Paradise' refers to 'God's garden,' an eschatological image of new creation. Jesus' promise of Paradise 'today' is in keeping with Luke's understanding

Amazing *Assurance*

of the immediacy of salvation (cf. 4:21; 19:9) and underscores a central aspect of Luke's perspective on Jesus' death: God's plan comes to fruition through, not in spite of, the crucifixion of Jesus, so that Jesus is able to exercise his regal power of salvation in death as in life" (Green, *The Gospel of Luke*, pp. 822, 823).

What difference does Jesus' assurance make when you or a loved one faces death?

The Fattened Calf: It is really significant that throughout the Jewish Scriptures, the atoning, substitutionary death of the Savior has been illustrated by the death of an animal, many times a calf or bull (see the Day of Atonement, Leviticus 16:3, 6, 11, 14, 15, 18, 27). Jesus was that Sacrifice for the atoning of sins. The father in the parable of the prodigal son uses the same word that in the Greek Old Testament was used for the bulls of the Day of Atonement. In the parable of the prodigal son, the "fattened calf" (Luke 15:23) would be killed and the celebration would begin! Jesus was dying that we may have a place in the Father's household! Oh, my soul, REJOICE! My heart burns within me . . . and I receive, once again, the assurance of my salvation through His blood!

Why do you think there are so many celebrations in Jesus' *lost and found* parables? (See Luke 15:6, 9, 23, 24.)

Let's reflect

One of the most inspiring stories that I have heard in the last few decades is the account of a father-son team, Dick and Rick Hoyt, who run marathons together. The amazing thing about them is the fact that the son, Rick, is a spastic quadriplegic with cerebral palsy. Most remarkably, every time they participate in a race, his father, Dick, pushes him in a wheelchair all the way to the finish line. It all started in 1977, when Rick, then a young man, asked his father to help him participate in a five-mile benefit run for a lacrosse player who was paralyzed in an accident.

His father agreed and pushed Rick in a wheelchair. When they had finished that first race, Rick wanted to say something to his dad, but he can't talk, so he had to wait until they got home. Once they arrived, he could communicate because, even though he can't control his extremities and lips, he has a headpiece attached to his chair through which he can type into a computer in order to communicate. He wrote down, "Dad, when I'm running, it feels like I'm not handicapped." Dick got so excited about this new discovery that he started training systematically, so that his son could participate in many races. He gave his son the *assurance* that he would bring him to the finish line every time. Since that first run, they have participated in many races and are still running today. If you want to learn more about this amazing family, visit their Web site at www.teamhoyt.com. You will be enchanted by photos of Rick's smile as they run. And it is heartwarming to see Dick's efforts as he works so hard to help his son, who can't run for himself. For me, the story came to a climax when I saw a documentary on the Hoyt team participating in the Ironman Triathlon in Hawaii. The father took his son through 112 miles of biking, 26.2 miles of running, and 2.4 miles of swimming so that Rick might experience the thrill of the race and know that he is worth every bit of Dick's effort! Rick will always be a winner, not because he is a strong and able athlete, but because his father, Dick, always takes him to the finish line! And he lives with that assurance. Their story has become a powerful enacted parable for me, demonstrating the way my salvation is achieved.

Write a story from your daily life that comes to mind in this session:

Why do you think Jesus gave such an outrageous response to the thief on the cross?

What is the evidence that a Christian is living with the assurance of salvation secured by Jesus at the cross?

First comes the crown of thorns, then the crown of glory. Jesus was crowned with glory and honor *because* of His suffering and death (Hebrews 2:9). What is the relationship between the Cross and the kingdom?

Repeat these words of Scripture aloud:

> *"Therefore, brethren, since we have confidence*
> *to enter the holy place by the blood of Jesus . . .*
> *let us draw near with a sincere heart in*
> full assurance *of faith"*
> (Hebrews 10:19–22; emphasis added).

Amazing *Assurance*

Let's comprehend Jesus in Scripture

Please take a moment to read Luke 23:42, 43. We will distinguish four sections in Jesus' response to the criminal on the cross. But before we go to these sections, let's review the order of the words in the original Greek because that will help us determine the force of each word in the sentence. The original Greek reads with the following word order:

"Truly to you I say today with Me you will be in paradise."

Now, let's analyze the four sections in Jesus' response:

Today. Jesus didn't want this man to wonder about his fate until Jesus came into His kingdom. No! This criminal could have the assurance of salvation *today,* at that very moment, without waiting one more second. No anxiety, no uncertainty. Just assurance . . . today.

The word *today* highlights the immediacy of the assurance of salvation throughout Jesus' ministry, remember? "Today this Scripture has been fulfilled in your hearing" (Luke 4:21; see also 19:9).

You will be. The assurance is given in the second person singular in the future tense and it is a *sure* thing! *You will be.* Not, *you might be,* nor, *let Me think if you will be.* That very day, God's child could have the assurance that he was going to spend eternity with his Father, in his Father's household. This was not the end for him, even though it surely looked like it. His presence with Jesus in His kingdom was not just a *possibility*. It was a *reality*!

Paradise. Jesus said, "You will be in Paradise"! Paradise! Remember? The nursery God made for His children! The place He created for their delight! The special Garden, in the middle of which you can find the tree of life! Remember? The very place God's children lost back in Genesis 3? This criminal is the first to be promised a bite from the fruit of the tree of life! He will be in *Paradise*! The Greek word used in Genesis 2 and 3 is *paradeisos* (the New Testament writers, when referencing the Old Testament, used the Greek translation of it, called the Septuagint or LXX). This is the place! Back with the Creator. This is the *only* time in all four Gospels that Jesus utters the word *Paradise*. At this very moment, He was opening up a way back home for His children, the way back to the tree of life, while taking upon Himself the death penalty they deserved. He had chosen to offer His perfect life (which none of us has) as a ransom for His children. And now, He could promise *Paradise*! And His *undeserving son* was the first recipient of that promise. Surprise! Paradise! The way home has been reopened.

With Me. Perhaps you noticed that I have intentionally skipped this

Amazing Grace

phrase so far. In Greek, the weight of the content is in the middle of the sentence. I wanted to leave this important middle part—"with Me"—to the last. Jesus is saying to him, "My undeserving child: all of the above is true for one reason: you will be *with Me*. You will be in Paradise *because* you are with Me. The best robe is MY ROBE of righteousness placed on you, even though you do not *deserve* it. Do you understand? That is why it is in the middle of the sentence . . . I AM your assurance!"

Let's respond to God's amazing assurance

I am an *undeserving* child of God, and yet I live with full assurance of salvation. He has embraced me, kissed me, and has clothed me with His robe of righteousness. I have sandals on my feet because I am a child of the King. I have prayed the prodigal criminal's prayer, and I have received the same assurance that he got that day. And you will receive the same response! If you have accepted Jesus as your personal Savior, you can live with the assurance of salvation that He Himself gave the criminal on the cross. If you haven't yet, please pause now and accept His death and resurrection on your behalf. Now we are ready to respond in gratitude, dedicating our lives to His glory. Please complete this *stem* exercise by writing different endings to the following sentence: "I accept Jesus' assurance because . . ."

I live within the paradox of two realities: I am *undeserving* and I am *saved* through Jesus Christ my Lord. He did for me what I could not do for myself! Join me in choosing FAITH over FEAR. You can live with the *amazing assurance* that you will be with Jesus in Paradise. And that assurance is with us at all times. Let me share with you my favorite childhood verse:

"God is our refuge and strength, *a very present help* in trouble. Therefore *we will not fear,* though the earth should change and though the mountains slip into the heart of the sea" (Psalm 46:1, 2; emphasis added). Yes! He is not only present, He is the *very present help.* Be assured!

> Take a moment to write your decision to live a life of assurance in Christ. Vow in your heart to reject a religion based on fear, because God's "perfect love casts out fear!" (1 John 4:18).

Amazing Reunion

Lesson 9

Let's start by reading Matthew 24:1–14, 29–31 and Revelation 19:11–16. As you read the biblical narrative, highlight words or phrases that catch your attention.

What is the most surprising part of the description of the second coming of Christ?

Let's study

The last book of the Bible is the revelation of Christ as the ultimate Redeemer, victorious against the kidnapper. The book is introduced as the unveiling of Jesus: "The *Revelation of Jesus Christ,* which God gave Him to show to His bond-servants, the things which must soon take place; and He sent and communicated it by His angel to His bond-servant John" (Revelation 1:1; emphasis added). In this book, the kidnapper is exposed. "And the great dragon was thrown down, the serpent of old who is called the devil and Satan, who deceives the whole world" (Revelation 12:9). Remember the *serpent* that *deceived* the children of God back in Genesis 3? We know exactly who the kidnapper is, and he is about to be no more.

This revelation (*apokalupsis,* which means "unveiling" or "disclosure") of Jesus is the last word of the Bible. It is written in apocalyptic style: a narrative genre that uses visualizations and symbols to convey the history of the plan of salvation from a cosmic perspective. It relates things from the past, things from the present, and things from the future (see Revelation 1:19). This literary genre was much more common during the time when the New Testament was written.

In many ways, this book is a summary of the Bible. In its English versions, it contains a little more than four hundred verses; but it has more than five hundred allusions to the Old Testament. This means that the author uses the main themes of the salvation history (for example, the plagues and the Exodus, the Exile and Babylon, and so forth) to demonstrate and announce the ultimate victory of our Redeemer over evil.

This book was written to encourage the faithful under difficult circumstances.

John announces to his readers that the final showdown between our Redeemer and the kidnapper is imminent. But if they hang in there until the end, believing in the Lamb who was slain, they will spend eternity with God.

This is a book of worship. Sixteen major worship scenes are portrayed in this unveiling narrative, where heaven and earth erupt in songs of exaltation, praising Him who has won victory through His blood. One of my favorite scenes of worship is the one narrated in Revelation 4 and 5. Could you pause for a moment and read both chapters?

Most of the book of Revelation is about waiting for the exciting moment when our *Go'el* comes back to take us to be with Him. Can you imagine waiting for a long, long time to see your children again? Our *Go'el* came to this world the first time in order to pay our ransom. His birth and death are narrated in the Gospels. The Cross was the moment when we were set free. His perfect life, death, and resurrection assured eternal life for all those who accept the *Go'el*'s payment on their behalf. Now, the Redeemer is coming back as a triumphant Victor to take us home with Him. The description of the event is breathtaking: "And I saw heaven opened, and behold, a white horse, and He who sat on it is called Faithful and True, and in righteousness He judges and wages war. His eyes are a flame of fire, and on His head are many diadems; and He has a name written on Him which no one knows except Himself. He is clothed with a *robe dipped in blood,* and His name is called The Word of God" (Revelation 19:11–13; emphasis added). What a triumphant view of our Redeemer! He hardly resembles here the suffering Jesus, the One who was humiliated and mocked! But there is one reminder of the costly ransom that He paid in the midst of such a spectacular portrayal of His second coming: He is wearing a *robe dipped in blood*. His blood was the price He paid. And we will forever remember.

Fill in the blanks with your own name, imagining what you would feel if Jesus returned now:

"For the Lord Himself will descend from heaven with a shout, with the voice of the archangel and with the trumpet of God, and the dead in Christ will rise first. Then _____, who is alive and remains, will be caught up together with them in the clouds to meet the Lord in the air, and so _____, and the rest of us, shall always be with the Lord. Therefore comfort one another with these words" (1 Thessalonians 4:16–18, paraphrased).

Let's understand

The Book of Revelation:
The last book of the Bible is the Revelation of Jesus Christ (see Revelation 1:1) from beginning to end. From a cosmic perspective, the author leads us to the conclusion of the great controversy between God and evil. It shows Jesus as the VICTOR, who, in spite of the Fall,

was able to redeem the human race. Yes, God wins! As mentioned before, this prophetic book is also a worship book, with more than sixteen glorious scenes of worship. This is one of my favorite worship scenes in the whole Bible, where the entire universe sings a new song to the Lamb who was slain:

> *"And I saw between the throne (with the four living creatures) and the elders a Lamb standing, as if slain, having seven horns and seven eyes, which are the seven Spirits of God, sent out into all the earth. And He came and took the book out of the right hand of Him who sat on the throne. When He had taken the book, the four living creatures and the twenty-four elders fell down before the Lamb, each one holding a harp and golden bowls full of incense, which are the prayers of the saints. And they sang a new song, saying,*
> *" 'Worthy are You to take the book and to break its seals; for You were slain, and purchased for God with Your blood men from every tribe and tongue and people and nation.*
> *" 'You have made them to be a kingdom and priests to our God; and they will reign upon the earth' "* (Revelation 5:6–10).

What a magnificent musical worship scene! Everybody singing about the achievements of Christ! I want to join in!

The book of Revelation, written in the apocalyptic genre and filled with meaningful symbols and numbers, offers a cosmic overview of human history.

"In the first chapter of the Revelation God identifies himself with the sentence, 'I am the Alpha and the Omega' (Rev. 1:8). In the final vision this is expanded to 'I am the Alpha and Omega, the first and the last, the beginning and the end' (Rev. 22:13). Alpha is the first letter in the Greek alphabet; Omega is the last. Alpha and Omega include between them all the letters. Anything written must use the letters of the alphabet. God is all the letters of the alphabet. . . . First and last are before us. The revelation is entire. The last word of scripture has the effect, then, of all well-made conclusions: it gives clarity and sense to the beginning and middle. What was unknown at the beginning, and unfinished in the middle, is now known and clear.

"The Revelation has 404 verses. In those 404 verses, there are 518 references to earlier scripture. If we are not familiar with the preceding writings, quite obviously we are not going to understand the Revelation. St. John has his favorite books of scripture: Ezekiel, Daniel, Zephaniah, Zechariah, Isaiah, Exodus. But there is probably not a single canonical Old Testament book to which he doesn't make at least some allusion. . . . St. John did not make up his visions of dragons, beasts, harlots, plagues, and horsemen out of his own imagination; the Spirit gave him the images out of the scriptures that he knew so well; then he saw their significance in a fresh way. Every line of the Revelation is mined out of rich strata of scripture laid down in the earlier ages" (Peterson, *Reversed Thunder*, pp. 22, 23).

The Second Coming: The second coming of Jesus is the great hope of the Christian faith. Having died in His First Advent in order to pay the ransom for humanity, Christ comes a second time to take us to be with Him forever. It means to receive the hug of our Creator we have been waiting for. It means the end of pain and death. It means to be with our Beloved, once again, as in the beginning. The description of Jesus' triumphant return is breathtaking, and I am sure that the prophet had a hard time finding the appropriate verbiage to communicate what he was shown.

Commenting on Revelation 19:11–13, Ranko Stefanovic helps us grasp the magnitude of the scene: "Once again John sees *heaven opened* as he did in Revelation 4:1. This time the door in heaven is not open for John to enter, but for Christ to come down to the earth. The warrior Christ is seen here as a Roman general riding on *a white horse* celebrating his triumph and victory. . . . The warrior Christ's *eyes were like a flame of fire.* This is reminiscent of his description in Revelation 1:14. The imagery signifies Christ's ability to judge; nothing can remain hidden from his penetrating insight. He wears on his head *many crowns.* These are royal crowns, signifying his royal power and authority to exercise judgment. The many crowns on his head stand in contrast to the crowns of the dragon in Revelation 12:3. In Revelation 5, Christ has been given authority to rule, but his rule was limited due to Satan's rebellious claim to dominion on the earth (cf. Luke 4:6). . . . Now, the downfall of end-time Babylon opens the door for Christ's definite right to rule. He is coming now as 'king of kings and Lord of lords' (Rev. 19:16) to destroy 'all rule and all authority and power' (1 Cor. 15:24) and become the King and Lord of all the kingdoms of the earth" (Stefanovic, *Revelation of Jesus Christ,* pp. 551, 552).

Let's reflect

Elizabeth was abducted from her own bedroom in Salt Lake City, on June 5, 2002, at the age of fourteen. Ed Smart, her father, went on television that same morning, pleading and begging the kidnapper to return his daughter. She was found nine months later on March 12, 2003, eighteen miles from her home. During the nine-month ordeal, the whole town was dressed up in blue ribbons, waiting for her safe return. Everyone was praying and hoping until that significant day when someone recognized Brian Mitchell from a sketch of the suspected kidnapper. I was grateful and relieved when she was found. The signs that were placed all over the town celebrating her homecoming touched me deeply. Businesses were not advertising their products on their commercial signs; you would only read "Elizabeth, Welcome Home" instead. I felt something very special when I read those signs, perhaps because it is also my name. Many times my mind went ahead to the day I will be reunited with my Creator and Redeemer. I imagined many signs in heaven with the same inscription: "Elizabeth, Welcome Home."

At the time of her rescue, I was deeply touched by her father's emotions and the statements he made. One of them is his response to a reporter who asked him to describe the first moments when he knew for sure that Elizabeth was alive. How can you describe such a scene? He said that he was in the police car, with Elizabeth in his arms, and he called his wife: "You are not going to believe this [he was sobbing as he related the dialogue]! Elizabeth is alive! And she is here in my arms!" When the interview was over, I imagined God talking about us. I imagined His excitement about our being rescued and reunited with Him forever. I had tears in my eyes when imagining Jesus, calling the Father, saying, "You are not going to believe this [sobbing]. Elizabeth is alive! And she is here in My arms!" Yes! We are going home!

Write a story from your daily life that comes to mind in this session:

Why is it of utter importance to understand that all Scripture points to the redemption achieved through Jesus and that God revealed His plans in a developmental and progressive manner?

What difference does it make for you to know that the cross is the core *hermeneutical* (interpretive) principle for understanding the Bible and God's covenant with us?

There are two dimensions to God's kingdom on earth that we Christians accept: "already" and "not yet." Jesus has already conquered death, but this reality is not yet fully realized on earth. How does a Christian manage to live in this in-between time, between Jesus' conquering of death and His coming back to take us home?

Repeat these words of Scripture aloud:

> "BEHOLD, HE IS COMING WITH THE CLOUDS,
> and every eye will see Him, even those who pierced Him;
> and all the tribes of the earth will mourn over Him. So it is to be. Amen.
> " 'I am the Alpha, and the Omega,' says the Lord God,
> 'who is and who was and who is to come, the Almighty' " (Revelation 1:7, 8).

Let's comprehend Jesus in Scripture

Jesus spoke about His second coming, and He told several parables about it: the parable of the slaves left in charge (Matthew 24:45–51); the parable of the virgins waiting for the bridegroom (Matthew 25:1–13); the parable of the slaves entrusted with talents (Matthew 25:14–30); and others. He wanted us to keep looking up and not get discouraged, even though we don't know the time of His coming. The fact that no one knows the time is repeated several times in a few verses: "But of that day and hour no one knows, not even the angels of heaven, nor the Son, but the Father alone" (Matthew 24:36; see 24:42; 25:13). Jesus mentioned many signs of His coming, so that we may know that the day is closer. The final sign, right before the Second Coming, is that the gospel will be preached in the whole world: "This gospel of the kingdom shall be preached in the whole world as a testimony to all the nations, and then the end will come" (Matthew 24:14).

The signs of the coming of Christ were never meant to frighten us, but to encourage us. I still remember a small group where we were discussing how the signs of His coming are like points on a map that reveal that the destination is coming closer. A wonderfully positive woman shared an insight that I will never forget. She told the group that when her children were young, they loved to visit their grandparents, and they had learned different landmarks along the way to know that they were getting closer. As they recognized these signs, they grew more and more excited, knowing that their much-awaited encounter with their beloved grandparents was at hand. Then she concluded: "This is the role of the signs of the second coming of Jesus. They are there so that we may recognize His closeness and get more and more excited!" I believe this with all my heart!

Even for the first generation of Christians, who, almost two thousand years ago, saw Jesus taken to heaven in front of their eyes, the news of Jesus' second coming was given as a source of hope and joy: "And after He had said these things, He was lifted up while they were looking on, and a cloud received Him out of their sight. And as they were gazing intently into the sky while He was going, behold, two men in white clothing stood beside them. They also said, 'Men of Galilee, why do you stand looking into the sky? This Jesus, who has been taken up from you into heaven, will come in just the same way as you have watched Him go into heaven' " (Acts 1:9–11). This promise of another coming of Jesus became known as the *parousia,* and it set the Christian community afire.

One of the most noticeable characteristics of those waiting for Jesus will be their rejoicing with the Bridegroom. Exploring the parable of the ten virgins, Ellen White ends her comments with a description of the amazing, indescribable rejoicing of that awaited encounter: "To His faithful followers

Christ has been a daily companion and familiar friend. They have lived in close contact, in constant communion with God. Upon them the glory of the Lord has risen. In them the light of the knowledge of the glory of God in the face of Jesus Christ has been reflected. Now they rejoice in the undimmed rays of the brightness and glory of the King in His majesty. They are prepared for the communion of heaven; for they have heaven in their hearts.

"With uplifted heads, with the bright beams of the Sun of Righteousness shining upon them, with rejoicing that their redemption draweth nigh, they go forth to meet the Bridegroom, saying, 'Lo, this is our God; we have waited for Him, and He will save us.' Isa. 25:9.

" 'And I heard as it were the voice of a great multitude, and as the voice of many waters, and as the voice of mighty thunderings, saying, Alleluia; for the Lord God omnipotent reigneth. Let us be glad and rejoice, and give honour to Him; for the marriage of the Lamb is come, and His wife hath made herself ready. . . . And he saith unto me, Write, Blessed are they which are called unto the marriage supper of the Lamb.' 'He is Lord of lords, and King of kings; and they that are with Him are called, and chosen, and faithful.' Rev. 19:6-9; 17:14" (White, *Christ's Object Lessons*, p. 421).

Let's respond to God's amazing reunion

When the disciples became a little anxious about some of the things Jesus was saying, He gave them the cure for a troubled heart: to remember His promise that He is coming back for us, to take us home. These words are meant for us as well.

Fill in the blank with your name:
Dear _____:
"Do not let your heart be troubled; believe in God, believe also in Me.
In My Father's house are many dwelling places; if it were not so,
I would have told you;
for I go to prepare a place for you. If I go and prepare a place for you,
I will come again and receive you to Myself, that where I am,
there you may be also.
And you know the way where I am going" (John 14:1–4).

Let your mind and heart focus on this promise. Let your thoughts and feelings take it all in. Now, write a letter to Jesus, letting Him know how eagerly you wait for the day of your reunion with Him! Let Him know that you truly trust in His promise to come again for you.

_____
_____
_____
_____
_____
_____
_____
_____
_____
_____

We have the great hope of the Second Coming. It will be an *amazing reunion* with our Creator and Redeemer. I can't wait. The last red letters in the Bible (direct words of Jesus) are recorded in Revelation 22:20 when the risen Christ speaks for the last time: "Yes, I am coming quickly." Do you hear the eagerness of a Parent coming back for His children? John's answer is also representative of the longing response all of us have to see our Redeemer and be with God forever: "Amen. Come, Lord Jesus" (verse 20).

Please take a moment to write your acceptance of the blessed HOPE of the SECOND COMING of Christ to take you home! May this reality that you accept by faith today guide your life until you see Jesus face-to-face!

Amazing *Reunion*

Amazing Restoration

Lesson 10

Read Revelation 21:1–7, 22, 23; 22:1–5, 12–14. As you read the biblical narrative, highlight words or phrases that catch your attention.

Write down the most amazing phrase in this whole narrative, and give the reason why you chose it.

___

Let's study

After a period of time specified as the "thousand years," the kidnapper, the serpent, "the devil who deceived them" (Revelation 20:10) is destroyed forever. Then the earth is re-created and becomes the new earth (see Revelation 21). It is very significant that our permanent home will be the same place we were at the beginning, because this was one of the roles of the kinsman-redeemer. Remember how he had to redeem property that was given up by a poor relative? "If a fellow countryman of yours becomes so poor he has to sell part of his property, then his nearest kinsman [*Go'el*] is to come and buy back what his relative has sold" (Leviticus 25:25). Jesus, our Kinsman-Redeemer, not only rescued us through the ransom He paid, but He also got our land back (the earth) as well. Oh, this is just so exciting and wonderful! Beyond words! The Bible comes full circle through the blood of the Lamb!

As we open the book of Revelation, we immediately get into the language that was used at the beginning of the Jewish Scriptures; for example, "to him who overcomes, I will grant to eat of the *tree of life* which is in the *Paradise* of God" (Revelation. 2:7; emphasis added). *Tree of life* and *Paradise* are words we encountered in Genesis 2, when God prepared the ultimate "nursery" for His beloved children. The tree of life is also present in Genesis 3, with the sad reminder that human beings would no longer have access to it because they were now mortals. But as we get to the place where the cosmic view of Jesus' ministry is unveiled, we start hearing this type of language again. When we start reading Revelation 21,

John announces that he "saw a new heaven and a new earth; . . . and there is no longer any sea" (verse 1). For the first-century Mediterranean world, the sea was the place where evil resided. Evil is no more. And a loud voice from the throne is heard. This voice announces the fulfillment of the ongoing covenant theme that was spoken at different times and in different ways all through the Bible, always pointing to God dwelling with His people (Revelation 21:3, 4). The presence of God with His people has been the theme throughout the history of humankind. They were created to be with Him. We are reminded of this throughout the Old Testament. "I will make My dwelling among you. . . . I will also walk among you and be your God, and you shall be My people" (Leviticus 26:11, 12).

Moreover, God designed a way in which His people would experience His presence: the tabernacle in the wilderness and, eventually, the temple. God manifested the glory of His presence in these sacred structures. When Jesus became flesh, He *tabernacled* (it is the same word *tabernacle,* only in verb form, usually translated as "dwelt") among us, and once again "we saw His glory, glory as of the only begotten from the Father, full of grace and truth" (John 1:14). Jesus was the ultimate representation of God's glory (see Hebrews 1:1–3). In the new earth, the tabernacle of God is among men because He is dwelling with them forever more. There is no more temple because God Himself is among them: "I saw no temple in it, for the Lord God the Almighty and the Lamb are its temple" (Revelation 21:22). God is finally back with His children, whom He lost in Paradise. The covenant of God was given to Adam, Noah, Abraham, Moses, and David in the Jewish Scriptures. These men of old received signs of the covenant and had glimpses of its developmental nature. When we get to the new earth, the covenant will be fulfilled, and the ultimate reality for us will be that we will have received the *divine sonship.* We are, in fact, children of God! God will be with us, and we will be with God! Reunited! Forever! The accomplishment of this final reality will be announced by God Himself (see Revelation 21:7).

Can you imagine the scene when we get to see what John saw? Fill in the blanks with your name:

"Then _____ saw a new heaven and a new earth; for the first heaven and the first earth passed away. . . . And _____ heard a loud voice from the throne, saying, 'Behold, the tabernacle of God is among men, and He will dwell among them, and they shall be His people, and God Himself will be among them' " (Revelation 21:1–3).

Let's understand

New Earth and Paradise:
The last book of the Bible ends with a scene of redeemed humanity, returned to the tree of life. We have come full circle: "Then he showed me a river of the water of life, clear as crystal, coming from

the throne of God and of the Lamb, in the middle of its street. On either side of the river was the tree of life, bearing twelve kinds of fruit, yielding its fruit every month; and the leaves of the tree were for the healing of the nations" (Revelation 22:1, 2). The same tree that God planted in Paradise in the beginning is back. Remember how Jesus promised Paradise to the criminal on the cross? Here we are, standing by the tree of life. Its fruit is described in vivid and luscious words. Then John utters the seventh and last beatitude in this book: "*Blessed* are *those who wash their robes,* so that they may have *the right to the tree of life,* and may enter by the gates into the city" (Revelation 22:14; emphasis added). The expression of "washing their robes" has already been explained previously in Revelation: "They have *washed their robes* and made them white *in the blood of the Lamb*" (Revelation 7:14; emphasis added). Those who are now the blessed ones have the right to the tree of life, a symbol of immortality, *because* they have washed their robes in the blood of the Lamb; they accepted the ransom paid by their *Go'el.* This is the *only* reason why they have the right to go back to the tree of life, which humans lost when they followed the kidnapper.

"Clearly one tree is on both sides of the river. This is an allusion to the Garden of Eden with the tree of life on the bank of the river flowing from the garden (Gen. 2:9). To eat from the tree of life in Eden meant 'to live forever' (Gen. 3:22). It was after Adam and Eve were banished from the garden that they were forbidden to approach the tree of life and eat from it (Gen. 3:23-24). The tree of life in the new Jerusalem symbolizes eternal life free of death and suffering. On the new earth—the restored garden of Eden—the tree of life is no longer forbidden; it is located in the midst of the new Jerusalem, and all the redeemed have access to it. Once again human beings will share in the gift of eternal life that Adam enjoyed before sin entered the world. All that was lost through Adam is now regained through Christ" (Stefanovic, *Revelation of Jesus Christ,* pp. 592, 593).

Covenantal Phrase and God's Presence With Us:

We have studied how God made a covenant to rescue His children and how, throughout the ages, He kept providing ever new information about this covenant. God constantly kept uttering the phrase that reminded us of His commitment to humankind: "I will be their God, and they will be My people." As we mentioned in the previous section, this phrase is used many times throughout the Old Testament as well (see Leviticus 26:11, 12). The fact that we will be back with God in an intimate communion is highlighted by the use of possessive pronouns: "He will dwell among them, and they shall be *His* people, and God Himself will be among them" (Revelation 21:3; emphasis added). One early manuscript reads, "and be *their* God," which is consistent with previous occurrences of this phrase (see Leviticus 26:11 and Ezekiel 37:27).

"He is *their* God (cf. Ezek. 36:28; Heb. 11:16). There is an intimate bond.

In Ezekiel's vision the name of the city was given as 'THE LORD IS THERE' (Ezek. 48:35). John writes of the fulfillment of what the prophet saw" (Morris, *Revelation,* p. 238).

Commenting on Revelation 21:3, 4, Stefanovic adds: "The redeemed on the new earth *will be his peoples.* This is the promise that was originally given to the people of Israel: 'I will make My dwelling among them. . . . I will also walk among you and be your God, and you shall be My people' (Lev. 26:11-12; cf. Exod. 29:45; Jer. 30:22). 'My dwelling place also will be with them; and I will be their God, and they will be My people' (Ezek. 37:27). John switches the singular 'people' to the plural 'peoples.' The plural form indicates the inclusion of all God's children from all ages—'from every nation and tribe and people and tongue' (Rev. 7:9)—in the population of the new earth" (Stefanovic, *Revelation of Jesus Christ,* p. 577).

He is our God, and we are His people, and He is with us! This intimate bond that we had from the beginning with God, as He came to visit His children in the Garden of Eden (Genesis 3:8), is a reality once again in the new earth. He has always been and will always be for us, "Immanuel: God with us." In his Gospel, Matthew tells us that Jesus was the embodiment of the Presence of God with us. "Now all this took place to fulfill what was spoken by the Lord through the prophet: 'BEHOLD, THE VIRGIN SHALL BE WITH CHILD AND SHALL BEAR A SON, AND THEY SHALL CALL HIS NAME IMMANUEL,' which translated means, 'GOD WITH US' " (Matthew 1:22, 23). And he ends his Gospel with Jesus' words that remind us of His presence with us until the very end: "I am with you always, even to the end of the age" (Matthew 28:20). In Revelation 21:3, we realize that His Presence is with us forever, and that He fulfilled His promise to be with us all the way through our journey back home. He never left us . . . because LOVE NEVER ENDS.

Let's reflect

I have good news and bad news for you. Which one do you want first? I usually want the good news first, hoping that it will outweigh the bad news that follows. "Even though it is cancer, it is curable; that's the good news." Well . . . praise the Lord! Thank You! Thank You! So what's the bad news?

It all started on Mother's Day 2011. My parents, my husband, and I were celebrating the special day in a restaurant. In the middle of the meal, my dad showed us an unusual swelling on his neck. He casually mentioned that he must have strained a muscle or something, but the swelling had grown to a golf-ball size within the last four days. I made him promise that he would go to the doctor that week. You see, he, like my mother, is a cancer survivor. He had already survived two types of cancer and was doing great. The results came back, and the unthinkable was happening. He now had a third type of cancer;

it was located in the lymphatic system, but we didn't know much more than that. After several tests and a biopsy, the good news and the bad news came in. The good news was that the chances of survival were great; it was considered a pretty curable cancer. Science had advanced in this area of cancer treatment, and the percentages presented to us were on his side. What about the bad news? He would have to suffer through several months of heavy and difficult chemotherapy. Much suffering awaited him throughout the upcoming months, pretty much for the whole year. But the good news far outweighed the bad news: when the suffering was over, the cancer would probably be gone! As I write these Bible study guides in 2014, my father is cancer free, and the only news left is the good news! And once again, I praise the Lord!

The book of Revelation (of Jesus Christ) unveils the final outcome, and it is really good news: we will be back in Paradise! And this is not just probable good news; it's for sure through the blood of the Lamb! Because of sin, humanity would go through suffering and difficulties, but the good news far outweighs the bad news! The last word of the Bible is there to encourage us!

Write a story from your daily life that comes to mind in this session:

God gave us the gift of the weekly Sabbath celebration on the seventh day (like a weekly Jubilee—see lesson 4) to remind us that He, our Creator, is also our Redeemer, our Deliverer, and our Provider, and that we can REST in His ability to take us back to Paradise. Read the following verses in detail: Genesis 2:2, 3; Exodus 16:29, 30; Exodus 20:8–11; Deuteronomy 5:12–15; Matthew 11:28–12:8; Hebrews 4:8–10. Why do we need a constant reminder to trust our *Go'el* and rest in His ability to rescue us and our land?

What does the weekly Sabbatical Feast of Remembrance have to do with the new earth (see Isaiah 66:23)?

We are living between Creation and re-creation. Why do we need a weekly Christ-centered REST on the seventh day?

Repeat these words of Scripture aloud:

*"Come to Me, all who are weary and heavy-laden,
and I will give you rest. Take My yoke upon you and learn
from Me, for I am gentle and humble in heart, and
YOU WILL FIND REST FOR YOUR SOULS.
For My yoke is easy and My burden is light"*
(Matthew 11:28–30; emphasis added).

Let's comprehend Jesus in Scripture

Let's read once again Revelation 21:22, 23: "I saw no temple in it, for the Lord God the Almighty and the Lamb are its temple. And the city has no need of the sun or of the moon to shine on it, for the glory of God has illumined it, and its lamp is the Lamb." I have always been so intrigued by these statements: the Lamb is the temple and the light.

The fact that Jesus is the **Light** of the world has been developed by many authors, especially by John in his Gospel, starting from the very beginning (see John 1:1–5). The Word was God and was the active Agent of creation. He Himself was Life (see John 1:4). He didn't just *give* life, but He *was* Life. And following the order of Creation, John talks about light (see Genesis 1:3–5); he says that the Word was life, and that life became "the Light of men" (John 1:4). And just as in the process of Creation, when the Light appeared, darkness was exposed (verse 5; see also John 3:18–21).

John goes on to say that Jesus "was the true Light which . . . enlightens every man" (John 1:9). Every person has the chance to accept or reject the Light. Then we learn that when the Light came home, those at home did not receive Him. What a tragedy! Home is supposed to be your own place, where everybody knows your name. The Word, the Life-Giver, and Light Bearer "was in the world, and the world was made through Him, and the world did not know Him. He came to His own, and those who were His own did not receive Him" (verses 10, 11). This is the bad news. But there is also good news. Some did accept the Light. And to those who received Him by believing in Him, He gave a gift: a new status—children of God. In one of His "I AM" statements found in this Gospel, Jesus boldly claims, "I am the Light of the world; he who follows Me will not walk in the darkness, but will have the Light of life" (John 8:12; see also John 9:5). In Revelation, John reveals that the Lamb is the lamp in the New Jerusalem (Revelation 21:23). Jesus illumines us from Genesis to eternity!

John, in his Gospel, also develops the theme that Jesus is the tabernacle of God. "The Word became flesh, and dwelt among us, and we saw His glory, glory as of the only begotten from the Father, full of grace and truth" (John 1:14).

The words used in this verse are of the utmost importance. First, John's choice of the word *flesh* is designed to highlight the fact that the Word did not make just a spiritual appearance but had a real physical body. Jesus is fully God and fully man. Second, the word *dwelt* means that He encamped or, in the Old Testament vernacular, *tabernacled* among us. This is a key word because it derives from the root word *tabernacle,* the sanctuary in the wilderness, the place where God's presence resided with His people. John wants his readers to catch the connection and to understand that the term refers back to the tabernacle that Moses built in the wilderness. Right afterward, he uses another word, *glory,* which also comes from the tabernacle vocabulary: "Then the cloud covered the tent of meeting, and the glory of the Lord filled the tabernacle" (Exodus 40:34). Now the tabernacle is the flesh, and we see God's glory through Jesus Christ. He is the fullest revelation of the glory of God. Furthermore, His utmost glory is the Cross, where God is revealed most fully. When humanity sinned, God found a way to continue His relationship with us, and He developed the idea of the tabernacle/sanctuary/temple, so that, through the services and sacrifices performed there, He could demonstrate His plan for us, and we could understand Jesus' redemption on our behalf. When Jesus came to earth, He *tabernacled* among us, and we saw more clearly the glory of God. When Jesus ascended to heaven, He left the members of His church as *temples* through which His glory may be revealed. Now in the New Jerusalem, the Lamb is the temple forever! He is truly Immanuel, God with us! He wants to be close to us! Forever!

Let's respond to God's amazing restoration

It is impossible to describe the new earth adequately. We can just imagine the voice declaring all of the benefits that will be ours when God dwells with His children forever. Think about it: just the abolishment of the effects of sin alone should make your heart soar—death, crying, and pain—they are all history!

The Bible ends with an invitation, and I want to extend it to you. It is the most important decision of your life: come to Jesus, accept Him as your personal Savior, and become His disciple. "The Spirit and the bride say, 'Come.' And let the one who hears say, 'Come.' And let the one who is thirsty come; let the one who wishes take the water of life without cost" (Revelation 22:17). So the question is, Do you want to accept His sacrifice on your behalf and embrace your new identity as a child of God? Do you wish to take the Water of Life without cost? If you do, please respond below, with a written confession of your faith in Jesus as your *Go'el* and His ability to rescue you and your land. He paid His life for your eternal life, so that you may receive it without cost.

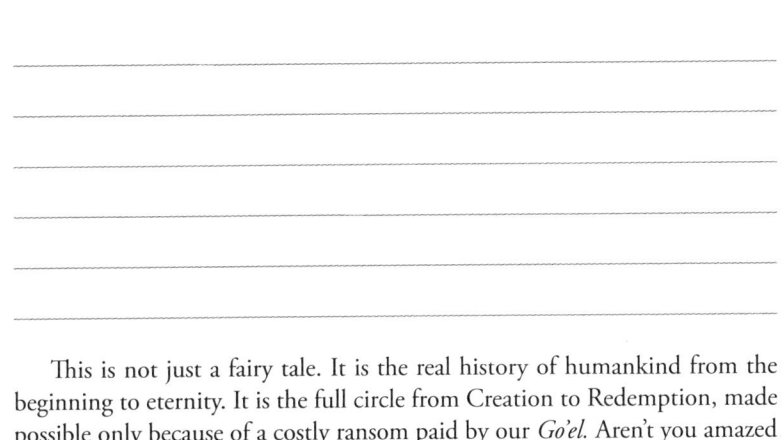

_____

_____

_____

_____

_____

_____

This is not just a fairy tale. It is the real history of humankind from the beginning to eternity. It is the full circle from Creation to Redemption, made possible only because of a costly ransom paid by our *Go'el*. Aren't you amazed by *this much* love? This is the story of the truly unexpected and *successful* rescue of God's kidnapped children. The *restoration* of paradise is assured through Jesus' blood. Forever, and ever, and ever, we will be studying the *amazing grace* of God, who simply refused to go through eternity without us, His beloved children. And we already know the end of the story:

And God and His children lived happily ever after!

The End
Amen!

Take a moment to write your thanksgiving and acceptance of God's promise to fully RESTORE our home with Him in the new earth. What difference that this make in your daily life from now on?

An Invitation

I am thankful to God for our journey together through His Word and for the plan of redemption that Jesus Christ carried out for each one of us! Now that we have been introduced to His AMAZING GRACE, I would like to extend to you a most important invitation.

In our lesson 5, we learned that Isaiah 53 has been called the "proto gospel," the first detailed indication that Jesus would die in our place:

> "Surely our griefs He Himself bore, And our sorrows He carried;
> Yet we ourselves esteemed Him stricken, Smitten of God, and afflicted.
> But He was pierced through for our transgressions, He was crushed for our iniquities;
> The chastening for our well-being fell upon Him, And by His scourging we are healed.
> All of us like sheep have gone astray, Each of us has turned to his own way;
> But the Lord has caused the iniquity of us all to fall on Him.
> He was oppressed and He was afflicted, Yet He did not open His mouth" (Isaiah 53:4–7).

Interestingly enough, in the first century A.D., when the new Christian church was just starting to form, this was the exact passage that an Ethiopian man was reading while traveling in his chariot. In Acts 8:25–39, you can read this fascinating story (Isaiah 53:4–8, compare it with Acts 8:32, 33). The Holy Spirit sent Philip to explain the good news of Jesus Christ to this man: "Then Philip opened his mouth, and beginning from *this Scripture* he preached Jesus to him" (Acts 8:35; emphasis added). And as soon as this man understood the good news of the gospel of Jesus Christ, he wanted to respond and asked to be baptized! "As they went along the road they came to some water; and the eunuch said, 'Look! Water! What prevents me from being baptized?'" (verse 36). As soon as the Ethiopian man understood the gift of God, he wanted to accept it and give a public testimony about his decision: "he ordered the chariot to stop; and they both went down into the water, Philip as well as the eunuch, and he baptized him. When they came up out of the water, the Spirit of the Lord snatched Philip away; and the eunuch no longer saw him, but went on his way *rejoicing*" (verses 38, 39; emphasis added).

Joy, joy, joy! That is the result of accepting by faith our salvation in Christ. And I want to invite you, too, to experience the joy of salvation by accepting the gift of heaven and becoming a disciple of Jesus. Baptism is the way we publicly acknowledge our acceptance of Jesus' life, death and resurrection on our behalf. As the apostle Paul explains: "do you not know that all of us who have been baptized into Christ Jesus have been baptized into His death? Therefore we have been buried with Him through baptism into death, so that as Christ was raised from the dead through the glory of the Father, so we too might walk in newness of life" (Romans 6:3, 4). If you have never been baptized, or even if you have been baptized but without a clear understanding of your salvation by the *amazing grace* of God through the salvific death of Christ on the cross, I urge you to make this decision now. Jesus stated that we become His disciples by participating publicly in the act of baptism (please take a moment to read Jesus' last words in Matthew 28:18–20), and I pray that you may make this decision as soon as possible!

This is an invitation for you to receive eternal life as a free gift of God in Christ Jesus, our Lord (Romans 6:23)! May you decide to accept Jesus into your life and through baptism join your Christian brothers and sisters who live and will continue to live eternally in AWE of His AMAZING GRACE!

Bibliography

Bruce, F. F. *The Epistle to the Hebrews.* Rev. ed. The New International Commentary on the New Testament. Grand Rapids, MI: Eerdmans, 1990.

———. *The New Testament Development of Old Testament Themes.* Grand Rapids, MI: Eerdmans, 1994. First published 1969 by Paternoster Press.

France, R. T. *The Gospel of Matthew.* The New International Commentary on the New Testament. Grand Rapids, MI: Eerdmans, 2007.

Green, J. *The Gospel of Luke.* The New International Commentary on the New Testament. Grand Rapids, MI: Eerdmans, 1997.

Hamilton, V. *The Book of Genesis: Chapters 1–17.* The New International Commentary on the Old Testament. Grand Rapids, MI: Eerdmans, 1990.

Hartley, J. *Genesis.* New International Biblical Commentary. Peabody, MA: Hendrickson, 2000.

———. *Leviticus.* Word Biblical Commentary. Nashville, TN: Thomas Nelson, 1992.

Keener, C. *The IVP Background Commentary: New Testament.* Downers Grove, IL: InterVarsity Press, 1994.

Lane, W. *The Gospel of Mark.* The New International Commentary on the New Testament. Grand Rapids, MI: Eerdmans, 1974.

Moo, D. *The Epistle to the Romans.* The New International Commentary on the New Testament. Grand Rapids, MI: Eerdmans, 1996.

Morris, L. *Revelation.* Tyndale New Testament Commentaries. Grand Rapids, MI: Eerdmans, 2000.

Nichol, F., ed. *The Seventh-day Adventist Bible Commentary,* 2nd ed. Vol. 1. Washington, DC: Review and Herald® Publishing Association, 1978.

Nolland, J. *The Gospel of Matthew.* The New International Greek Testament Commentary. Grand Rapids, MI: Eerdmans, 2005.

Oswalt, J. *The Book of Isaiah: Chapters 40–66.* The New International Commentary on the Old Testament. Grand Rapids, MI: Eerdmans, 1998.

Peterson, E. *Reversed Thunder: The Revelation of John and the Praying Imagination.* New York, NY: HarperCollins, 1991.

Stefanovic, R. *Revelation of Jesus Christ: Commentary on the Book of Revelation.* Berrien Springs, MI: Andrews University Press, 2002.

Strauss, M. *Four Portraits, One Jesus.* Grand Rapids, MI: Zondervan, 2007.

Stuart, D. *Hosea-Jonah.* Word Biblical Commentary. Nashville, TN: Thomas Nelson, 1987.

White, E. G. *Christ's Object Lessons.* Washington, DC: Review and Herald®, 1941.

———. *The Desire of Ages.* Mountain View, CA: Pacific Press® Publishing Association, 1940.

For FREE video streaming, audio books, biblical studies, books, DVDs, podcasts, and much more, download our Jesus 101 app on any device and find us at www.jesus101institute.com

If you have been blessed by this book and would like to help us keep spreading the good news of Jesus Christ through preaching, teaching, and writing, please send your donations to

Jesus 101

Jesus 101 Biblical Institute
P. O. Box 10008
San Bernardino, CA 92423

www.jesus101institute.com